Advanced Praise for *Singlehandedly*

"Ruth has spent her career championing diversity efforts through education, mentoring, and building opportunities for people from under-resourced communities. She brings honesty and vulnerability to the conversation on diversity through the lens of a person born with a disability—and opens minds on how to create greater inclusion. Her book *Singlehandedly* will surely inspire others in many ways."

—**Roger W. Ferguson, Jr.**, Immediate Past President and CEO, TIAA, and Former Vice Chairman of the Federal Reserve System

"For some of us, bringing our full self to our life and work presents unique challenges, and sometimes it begins with the acceptance and embracing of our own differences. Ruth Rathblott's powerful story of coming out of hiding to own her disability resonates deeply with me, as someone in the LGBTQ+ community who struggled with the closet for many years, only to discover the liberation on the other side. People with disabilities are a massive and diverse community who continue to be underrepresented in workforce inclusion strategies, with so many still hiding their disabilities. This must change so that institutions better reflect the reality of our world, and unleash all the potential that exists, in every community. As Ruth says, 'The more we share our stories, the more others feel comfortable sharing theirs.' Thank you, Ruth, for shining your light so that others may follow!"

—**Jennifer Brown**, Founder, Jennifer Brown Consulting; Author, *Inclusion, How to be an Inclusive Leader,* and *Beyond Diversity*; Podcast Host, *The Will to Change*

"*Singlehandedly* helps us expand our minds to include disability in the diversity conversation—and end its exclusion. Bravo!"

—**Caroline Casey**, Founder, the Valuable 500

"As someone who has been a long-time diversity and disability advocate, I applaud Ruth for sharing her lived experience as someone born with a disability and her journey from hiding to unhiding through her book *Singlehandedly*; she lends a critical voice to the conversation on expanding the diversity conversation to making it fully inclusive. Disability needs to be part of the diversity, equity, and social justice conversation. We cannot effectively challenge inequality—or advance our social justice mission—unless we address the needs, concerns, and priorities of the one billion people around the world who live with disabilities."

—**Darren Walker**, President, Ford Foundation

"*Singlehandedly* is a **must-read** if you are living with a disability, supporting a loved one with a disability, or just want to be a more inclusive and understanding human being. As leaders in Diversity, Equity, and Inclusion, we are always trying to turn compassion into real action and positive results. As Ruth eloquently points out in her speaking and now in her book, the idea is that disability cuts across all lanes of diversity; it doesn't discriminate. The book is an important "how to" guide to expand the conversation on diversity in the workplace. Sharing her story through the lens of someone with a disability, Ruth helps us begin reflecting on a deeper level about people's hidden differences and how we can help others unhide to create inclusive work environments. I applaud her for working to create awareness and support around difference, disability, and inclusion."

—**Julie Kae**, VP of Sustainability and DE&I,
Executive Director of Qlik.org

"As the founder of the Lucky Fin Project and mother of a daughter with a limb difference, I personally value Ruth's strong voice for the limb difference community—and beyond. Her book is about how being born a little differently doesn't stop us from accomplishing anything we set out to do—and the importance of finding community and connection. I applaud her for her vulnerability and strength in sharing her story."

—**Molly Stapleton**, Founder, The Lucky Fin Project

"As a constant advocate for individuality and striving to share the story of difference myself, I am grateful that Ruth shares with the world her journey from hiding her limb difference to unhiding and celebrating her whole self—her uniqueness. The power of her book is about self-acceptance and building community—as she finds, she can't do it *Singlehandedly*."

—**Sydney Mesher**, Trailblazer dancer, actor, author, and inclusion advocate

"*Singlehandedly* is a fascinating journey of accepting one's differences, embracing and appreciating those differences, and ultimately unhiding! Ruth, a very successful speaker with a visible disability, offers digestible vignettes and insights that allow us to fully understand what led her to go from hiding her disability from everyone around her, to sharing who she is with the world. As you turn each page Ruth's vulnerability and insight are overwhelmingly welcome. Reading this memoir is like making a new friend, someone you can really trust. Wherever you are on your journey of hiding part of yourself or looking for a little encouragement, this is the book you need. I highly recommend *Singlehandedly*."

—**Dr. Truett Lee Vaigenur, Jr**, York College LEADS Specialist, host of Disabilities Redefined, children's book author

"When I started Innovation Women, I was naïve. 'Get more women on stage,' I thought. I didn't understand that diversity and inclusion had to be more than race and gender. Ruth's story is the one you need to read to fully understand the true breadth and depth of diversity and inclusion. Why *is* disability missing from the diversity conversation? It's time to find out."

—**Bobbie Carlton**, Founder, Innovation Women

"Ruth has spent her career closing the opportunity gap for youth through access to education and opportunity by leading nonprofit organizations. She also offers her strong voice to expand the conversation on diversity through the lens of someone with a visible disability. Her insights and questions offer a powerful opportunity for us all to reflect deeply. *Singlehandedly* is an important guide in starting inclusion discussions."

—**Carol Argento**, President & CEO, Charles Hayden Foundation

"In *Singlehandedly*, Ruth is authentic, vulnerable, and transparent. She shares her lived experiences—hiding, not hiding, and then ultimately fully owning her disability and the power therein. She is walking in her courage to fully live her life and to use it as a tool to teach others how to own and expand the conversation from diversity to inclusion by owning your own difference and leveraging it to get to know and embrace others."

—**Carla Harris**, Wall Street veteran and author of *Expect To Win*

"Ruth shares powerful stories and insights to bring to life her journey of hiding her disability for 25 years. In these pages, she is both vulnerable and forceful, challenging us to open up a long-overdue conversation in our society, and inspiring others to follow her lead."

—**Adam Bryant**, managing director of The ExCo Group and author of *The CEO Test: Master the Challenges that Make or Break All Leaders*

"I have known Ruth for many years—initially through her leadership in the nonprofit sector, where she has created access to mentoring opportunities for young people through corporate employee engagement, and now through her professional speaking and authorship in expanding workplace diversity conversations. I am delighted to see her following her passion and sharing her vulnerability and strength with the world! *Singlehandedly* will help us all to reflect on our own differences and embrace the connections with others."

—**Karen Kelso**, Fortune 500 Global Philanthropy and
Social Impact specialist/executive

"Ruth is someone who embraces her full power. She has taken the thoughtful journey from hiding to discovering her uniqueness; she now shares those gifts with the world through her speaking and writing to empower others to see themselves fully."

—**Nell Merino**, Take Our Daughters to Work Day and Founder,
nellmerlino.com

"*Singlehandedly* is a vulnerable look at disability, our own perceptions, and how others view us. Ruth takes us on her journey from hiding to self-acceptance and then realizes she has a leadership role to play in disability inclusion and representation. There are lessons for all of us, whether our disability can be seen or not. Well done, Ruth."

—**Meg O'Connell**, CEO of Global Disability Inclusion

"Ruth's message about true inclusion and the critical reasons for including persons with disabilities in the workforce is a powerful read. We also need to consider the intersections of disability and diversity and come together with pride. We are all stronger together."

—**Debra Ruh**, CEO, Ruh Global IMPACT, and
Executive Chair of Billion Strong

"Storytelling is our most powerful communication tool. In *Singlehandedly*, Ruth uses this immense power to spark our curiosity, inform us, serve as a virtual reality simulator, and share values. Her stories deeply connect us, as she takes us on her heart-wrenching and heart-soaring journey to unhiding her disability and finding the power of authenticity and joy. Throughout the book, she shares powerful insights and asks critical questions about how we, as a society, both minimize and magnify disability. In doing so, she creates the space and time for us to reflect on our own stories. I celebrate her courage in unhiding—and her vulnerability in sharing her story as a role model for others to share theirs!"

—**Deborah V. Pagnotta**, Founder and Chief Visionary, ULUstory

"Ruth tells her powerful story about her 25-year journey from hiding her physical disability out of fear of rejection and judgment to ultimately embracing her difference. She reveals how she found freedom by allowing herself to be vulnerable and sharing her story with the world. Her journey can teach all of us valuable lessons about courage, hope, and acceptance of who we are."

—**Ron Claiborne**, former ABC News correspondent

"I have witnessed Ruth's growth in accepting her disability and her continuous advocacy on behalf of others. In her work, she shares how being vulnerable and owning your difference connects you with others. Ruth uses her voice to champion and inspire others."

—**Denise E. Harris**, ACC, Founder/CEO,
Denise Harris Executive Coaching & Corporate Consulting

"In *Singlehandedly*, Ruth beautifully recounts her story of hiding her limb difference and feeling intense angst as a teenager before finally accepting her differences and embracing her authenticity as a human being. On her journey, she also encounters and unveils a hierarchy around diversity and disability that exists. If you want to expand the conversation on diversity, this is a critical guide to start those conversations!"

—**Chris Meek**, Author of *Next Steps Forward*

"Ruth uses her voice as a professional speaker and now author to reinvent the conversation about diversity and include someone born with a physical disability. She is a courageous visionary. This book is a must-read!"

—**Jeanne M. Stafford,** Founder, Stafford & Company

"*Singlehandedly* touched my soul as I read about Ruth's life experiences relating to her left hand since I also was born limb unique. As little girls, I wish we had been friends, and our moms, too. My tears turned joyful for Ruth in her quest for freedom in unhiding and accepting her special hand. Ruth's vignettes are honest, courageous, and poignant. She brings you along in her journey to freedom! Ruth's book affirms the power of our words to each other and the importance of empathy and grace. I cheer for Ruth as she strives to encourage others in the limb difference community and beyond to talk about, accept, and embrace our differences which make each of us unique and memorable. Singlehandedly moved me and inspired me!"

—**Julie Sanders Keymer**, Vice President, The Bible In Living Sound

"Ruth reminds us all to be open, vulnerable, and step into our truth through her incredible journey of acceptance and the redefinition of inclusion and diversity. Touching beyond belief."

—**Cheryl Bayer**, CEO, Living Popups LLC

"Have you ever felt that you just don't belong—that you're the different one? Ruth Rathblott takes on this universal and powerful topic in her book, *Singlehandedly*, and offers insights for those who have been hiding their differences in an attempt to belong. This book is more than a memoir and more than a book on diversity—it is a tool for discussing inclusion in a way that has not yet been explored. Highly recommended."

—**Cathy Fyock**, Author, *The Speaker Author*

SINGLE
HANDEDLY

LEARNING *to* UNHIDE *and* EMBRACE CONNECTION

RUTH RATHBLOTT, MSW

Publishing support provided by
Ignite Press
5070 N. Sixth St. #189
Fresno, CA 93710
www.IgnitePress.us

ISBN: 979-8-9863847-0-2 (Paperback)
ISBN: 979-8-9863847-1-9 (Hardcover)
ISBN: 979-8-9863847-2-6 (E-book)
ISBN: 979-8-9863847-3-3 (Audiobook)

For bulk purchases, book clubs, and booking, contact:
Ruth Rathblott
ruth@ruthrathblott.com
ruthrathblott.com

Library of Congress Control Number: 2022910447

Cover design by Salman Sarwar
Edited by Elizabeth Arterberry, Christine Borris, and Charlie Wormhoudt
Interior design by Jetlaunch
Cover photos by Maggie Marguerite Studio

FIRST EDITION

THANK YOU

Mom and Dad.

Together, you charted unnavigated waters with very little external support.

Thank you for always believing in me, pushing me forward, and teaching me to find solutions.

I love you.

DEDICATION

Little Ruthie:
You needed someone to talk to about your difference.
You felt alone, afraid, and unsure of how to fit in.
You hid because that felt safe, and you found acceptance when you pretended.
You were strong and determined, but you struggled with how to love yourself fully.
You needed a mentor, someone to guide you toward self-acceptance.
I see you now.

And, for all those who need this book, wherever you are on your
journey, you, too, can unhide, connect, and be free.
You are not alone.

TABLE OF CONTENTS

INTRODUCTION

Hiding and Unhiding Defined for this Book

❖ **Hiding: turning inward**

Hiding: deliberately not sharing a part of yourself for fear that someone will judge, criticize, reject, and even make an assumption about you based on stigmas and stereotypes.

Hiding: accompanied by shame and loneliness; lacking a connection to yourself and others.

Hiding affects how you show up and how you act because you feel unsafe.

Synonyms: covering, lying, masking, passing, and concealing.

❖ **Unhiding: connecting outward**

Unhiding: sharing the most vulnerable parts of ourselves with others.

Unhiding: having courage and taking risks with psychological safety.

Unhiding: being seen, accepted, and authentic.

Unhiding: recognizing that our differences are our gifts and make us unique and beautiful. Our differences offer us perspective and the ability to transcend challenges.

Unhiding allows us to build understanding and empathy for someone else's challenge.

Synonyms: uncovering, sharing, finding freedom, coming out, and owning your difference.

The journey from Hiding to Unhiding is a continuum;
wherever you find yourself on it, it is okay.

Hiding <--> Unhiding

Why This Book?

What are you hiding?

You have covered parts of yourself from the world—perhaps your physical health, mental health, learning challenges, neurodiversity, gender, sexuality, ethnicity, family background, education, weight, politics, or financial status. You are afraid that you will face judgment, stigma, and rejection if others know your secret. You judge and criticize yourself, which leads you to cover up those things you don't want others to know because letting people know would only lead to questions and assumptions you don't feel like answering.

You feel alone like you are the only one hiding something.

You have lived your life as a con artist, not the type that breaks the law, but as someone who has hidden parts of yourself from others. Not because you want to deceive, but because you want others to believe that you are whole—you want to be accepted.

Me, too.

I was born with a limb difference—a little left hand.

For 25 years, my little hand rarely saw the light of day; instead, it was buried deep in the front pocket of my pants, hidden under extra-long sleeves, or carefully concealed behind a bag or under books. My hand was always out of sight. No one ever saw it. I pretended to have two fully developed hands wherever I went. I got really good at hiding.

I felt as though I had been on a deserted island by myself for much of life, never interacting with anyone who looked like me. I thought I was the only one in hiding. I refused the disability label, choosing instead to *pass* as "two-handed" and "able-bodied."

I fooled most people—friends, potential dates, work colleagues, supervisors. While some may say, "So what, this seems harmless," I unintentionally hurt people with my omission, using sarcasm, rigidity, and unreliability to keep people from getting too close to me. I built walls to protect myself that were so high and pushed people away because I carried so much shame. Hiding impacted my relationships deeply: the ones I have, the ones I never gave a chance to develop, and, most importantly, my relationship with myself.

I am sorry that I lied, but I felt I had no other choice at the time.

For half my life, hiding my hand affected what I thought about my beauty, ability, and worth. My obsession with hiding prevented me from enjoying daily life activities; I kept myself from doing things that involved exposing my hand, like sports, theater, and social activities. I became disengaged from my life. Hiding my hand even physically changed my body posture; my upper body leaned to the left to accommodate my hiding. I tried to unhide many times in my life, always promising myself I would stop hiding next time, the next date, the next new opportunity. Each small attempt to unhide felt like a triumph, but the defeat quickly came when I would immediately go back to hiding.

Over the past few years, I have been on a personal journey to find acceptance by learning to unhide. I have searched for and found community, connection, and love.

I write this book with the hope that, wherever you are on the journey of self-acceptance and unhiding, you will know that you are not alone and that there is a path to living life fully and loving your whole self; there are people waiting to support you. I also write this book to expand the definition of diversity and create more inclusive conversations.

Why Now?

Diversity is at the forefront of most people's minds. The death of George Floyd ignited global attention that made it possible for marginalized racial communities to have their voices heard finally.

Many companies responded by prioritizing Diversity, Equity, Inclusion, and Belonging (DEIB) initiatives, hiring dedicated staff, and enhancing (and, in some cases, reigniting) their diversity efforts with training and emerging employee affinity groups. The workplace conversations focused mainly on the traditional definitions of race and gender, with an occasional mention of sexual orientation. While these themes are critical pillars in the diversity and inclusion conversation, a considerable part of the population is left out: those with a disability—both visible and invisible.

According to the Centers for Disease Control (CDC), one in four American adults has a disability—that's 61 million people. Those with a disability, the visible and invisible (mental health and neurodiversity), are the largest minority group. Disability is true intersectionality. It cuts across all lanes of diversity: race, gender, and sexual orientation. You can be born with a disability or develop one at any point in your life—at any age. Many of us have and care for family members with disabilities. Disability doesn't discriminate; it touches all of our lives.

Because disability is often excluded in the diversity conversation, a massive percentage of the population is left out of those discussions. Exclusion has consequences, and it makes a statement. It says to the world that disability does not matter; it builds a hierarchy within diversity of what matters most and what is an afterthought; it devalues someone's experience of difference and challenge; and, finally, when a group is excluded from the dialogue, full representation cannot be achieved in that conversation.

It leaves us to wonder: who gets to define the diversity conversation?

Excluding people from spaces that celebrate and openly discuss diversity contributes to hiding. If we exclude you, the message is "we don't want to hear from you." So, people hide their disabilities. They hide for many reasons. Some are concerned that if they open up about their disability, it may negatively affect how others perceive them. They want to fit in because they fear judgment, rejection, ostracization, or being seen as different—and difficult.

The Americans with Disabilities Act (ADA) was passed in 1990, and since then, disability representation has grown significantly. There have been several recent noteworthy events that may have been overlooked, just a few to mention:

- In Government, Tammy Duckworth was the first woman with a disability elected to Congress and the first female double amputee in the Senate in 2016; in 2021, the State of New York created its first Chief Disability Officer.
- In Sports, the NFL drafted a player with a limb difference in 2018, Shaquem Griffin, and Carson Pickett became the first player with a limb difference in US Women's National Team for soccer in 2022.
- In the Arts, the Rockettes hired Sydney Mesher, the first person with a disability in its 100-year history, in 2019; Ali Stroker, the first actress in a wheelchair, won a TONY Award for Best Performance in *Oklahoma* in 2019; *Crip Camp* received an Academy Award nomination for Best Documentary Feature in 2020, and *CODA* won the Oscar Award for Best Picture, along with Troy Kotsur, the first deaf man to win an Oscar, for Best Supporting Actor, in 2022.

We still have many more mountains to climb concerning disability and accessibility, representation, workforce development, and policy. I look forward to an expanded list of accomplishments in the foreseeable future.

I lend my voice to the diversity and disability space by sharing my journey of hiding and unhiding as a tool to spark conversation.

Hiding parts of ourselves is pervasive, especially in the workplace, as evidenced in the Deloitte study[*] (2013), finding that 61 percent of people "cover" part of their identity in the workplace. I believe we must unhide to bring our best selves forward and find personal and professional self-acceptance.

There are so many questions we need to answer.

Why do so many of us hide parts of ourselves?
Are we expected to hide so that we will fit in?
Why don't we share our differences so we won't feel so alone?
How can we unhide and safely share that part of ourselves?
What is our incentive to unhide?
Why is disability missing from the diversity conversation?
And how can we redefine disability?

Disability is not a bad word; it's strong and powerful.

A Guide: How to Use This Book

In every good story we follow the arc of the classic hero's/heroine's journey—someone facing a challenge, finding a guide to help them conquer the obstacle, and then being presented with the next challenge. In the pages ahead, that's the essence of my story: my journey of hiding, feeling excluded, finding connection, and ultimately unhiding.

The stories are grouped so you can choose to read straight through or pick a topic you are curious to learn more about. I hope you can use it as a guide for conversations at home, work, in a book club, and throughout your network; it is also meant to be a resource for how leaders and teams can build inclusive work environments focused on belonging and acceptance.

---

[*] https://www2.deloitte.com/us/en/pages/about-deloitte/articles/covering-in-the-workplace.html

---

Insight: Each chapter is a collection
of short vignettes told in the
first-person, present tense. I offer
my insights and pose reflection
questions for things to consider
along your reading journey.

My suggestion for reading this is to start at the beginning with Chapter One, as it sets the framework for understanding me and why I hid my hand for so many years. As a note, I refer to my hand in several ways throughout the book: my little hand, missing hand, left hand, and limb difference. These are all terms I have personally used throughout my life.

Hiding looks different for everyone, and so does the path to unhiding. This book is a tool for reflection wherever you are on your path to self-acceptance and belonging. Just as hiding parts of yourself and creating limiting beliefs doesn't occur overnight, the process to unhide takes time. Unhiding is a personal coming-out process filled with many emotions and attempts.

By using my lived experience as someone who once hid her disability, I hope that you will use this book as a prompt to explore your own differences and work to create a space to embrace others' differences. I look forward to hearing what resonates with you and how you think we can expand the diversity, equity, inclusion, and belonging conversation together. Please reach out to me through my website: ruthrathblott.com.

PART ONE

HIDING

1

WELCOME TO MY WORLD

From the beginning.
Each of us has a start to our story, sometimes several
beginnings—several defining events that help shape who we
become. We hear messages that frame our experiences.

In this chapter:

I set the stage for understanding my experience by introducing you to
my hand and my beginning.

Step Inside

Oh my, what happened to your hand?
Was it an accident?

Did you cut it off yourself?
Does it hurt?

You have no hand.
It looks like you have half a hand.

Oh, you can't do that. Let me help you.
Can I pray for you so it will grow? God bless you.

If people know about your hand, they won't like you.
Why don't you just cover it up with a prosthesis?

You're not "that" disabled.
It's not really a disability.

I don't see you "that" way.
I forgot about your hand.
I didn't even notice it.

You shouldn't hide anything about yourself.
Oh my. You're so brave; you've overcome so much.

The words are often accompanied with:
Glances—strangers staring too long and double-takes.
Whispers—parents shushing kids who ask.
Touches—people grabbing my hand without permission.

Welcome to my world.

Meet My Little Hand

My little hand is beautiful, unique, resilient, and full of grace.

Two inches long, two inches wide, and five inches in circumference.

In elementary school, while other kids trace their fingers in the shape of turkeys for Thanksgiving decorations, I trace my little hand and imagine it looks like a little bear cub. Objectively, it probably looks more like a miniature pitcher's mitt.

My left hand exists as an extension of my forearm, angled straight down; my left arm is a hand length shorter than my other arm. The wrist is thin and can move back and forth in motion, but not side to side. A semicircular nub sits on my wrist with five mini nubs as outgrowths, representing places where the fingers would have grown. The thumb has a tiny nail that often attracts the attention of little kids. There is a slight indent mark, almost like an eye, between the thumb and index finger; you must look closely to see it.

My left hand has distinct palm lines; I never really noticed them until writing this book.

Insight: As we unhide, we learn how
to take better care of ourselves.

For many years, I hid my hand. I neglected it. Winters were the worst because I didn't know that I had to keep it especially warm, as it has less blood flow; as a result, my hand now has permanent frostbite.

I now realize my hand requires special attention and care as I unhide it. I bundle it up with a sock and a mitten in the winter to keep it warm;

I ask for moisturizing lotion and a massage when I get a manicure (I used to think I would be bothering the manicurist if I asked), and now, my hand gets plenty of vitamin D from the sun because it is out and exposed. I even use a tailor now to shorten my left sleeve on garments. My hand is no longer in hiding.

For much of my life, it served as an excuse for not living my life fully and often prevented me from connecting with others. Now, I see my hand as a natural radar detector for people, weeding out those who aren't good for me and bringing me community and kindness from those who are important. It's also something people remember about me; it distinguishes me and makes me unforgettable.

My hand has become a source of strength; it allows me to connect with people in unique and unexpected ways.

The first time I took a photo of my hand, on purpose, was when I was 49 years old, at a picnic for people with limb differences. Nervously and self-consciously, I put my hand forward to be part of something, to own it as my badge—my badge of courage, my badge of distinction, my badge of fitting in. It was the first time I was proud to show my hand because it meant I fit in; I wasn't "the other." I felt seen as whole.

Treat Her as Normal

My parents meet in a magical, romantic movie way while traveling abroad; they notice each other while standing in line at the Tower of London in England and imagine, with active inner dialogue, *That's the person I am going to marry*. They flirt, chat, and attend the theater together that afternoon, and then, that evening, walking back to my mother's hotel, my dad proposes marriage. My mom says yes.

My dad flies home to Philadelphia, and my mom heads home to San Francisco.

She immediately buys a one-way ticket to Philadelphia.

They marry in a judge's office with only a handful of my dad's family present. Their fantasy is to start a life together and raise a family.

After the first year, my mom gets pregnant; she has a relatively smooth pregnancy despite an emotional upset early on, for which she takes a "mild" sedative.

My mom has heavy contractions on the afternoon before my birth; they head to the hospital. Their birthing plan is considered radical for the time. Their doctor is one of the few medical professionals at that time who lets fathers into the delivery room. My mom insists on natural childbirth, no drugs, no epidural.

At 2:20 a.m. on June 26, I arrive. Eight pounds, five ounces. Healthy. A relatively smooth delivery, except for one thing. I was born in the days before sonograms, and I am born without a fully formed left hand, which is a total surprise to those in the delivery room.

Everyone goes into swift action.

The nurses quickly sweep me away under the guise of cleaning me up.

The doctor ushers my dad out of the room and tells him that his daughter was born with a "congenital birth defect," meaning my left hand is not fully formed. (The standard checklist for a healthy baby, ten fingers and ten toes, doesn't apply to me.) The doctor wants to let my dad know so that he can go and comfort my mom, as he imagines she will be in shock when she finds out.

My dad is back in the room, preparing to deliver the news.

A nurse notices the tension.
She speaks to them and comforts them with a gentle directive.

"You will take this little girl home, and you will treat her like you would any other child. You will love her and treat her as normal."

And that's exactly what they do.

They encourage me to try everything during my childhood. Crawling. Swing sets and jungle gyms. Tying my shoes and doing my own pony-tails. Riding a bike. Playing the trumpet and the drums. Acting in plays. They let me succeed, and they let me fail.

Still, as new parents, they search for answers and external support. This is in the days before the internet, so all information comes through word of mouth and through baby books, like Dr. Spock's *Baby and Child Care*. My parents want to ensure my healthy development. They put their trust in the medical community. But the doctors have no idea what caused my limb difference; many give misinformation and poor guidance. Some blame the prescription drug that my mom took for that earlier emotional episode. Others focus on the consequences that the "defect" will have long-term, such as the "science" behind calcu-lating my height based on the space between my wrist and hand, which would predict how tall I would be (in their estimation, eventually over six feet tall). Another medical theory focuses on a random bone near my ear that would cause fatal brain swelling. The medical staff have no real answers or concrete information about what caused my "birth anomaly."

Early on, the hospital staff provides my parents with information about a support group for parents of children with disabilities. My mom attends one session and quickly determines that it is not for her or for me. Most of the children in the group have significant, severe disabilities. Mine seems minor. She and my father are left alone in nav-igating these waters of supporting a child with a disability; they must independently determine what's best for their baby girl.

My parents worry but keep the nurse's words, "Treat her as normal," as a mantra close to their hearts—it's their guiding principle on how to raise me. They find it challenging to address the topic of my disability and generally try to act as if everything is fine, with a few attempts at "fixing" it.

My hand isn't talked about with me. I learn to act like it doesn't exist and that it's not important.

Nobody asks:
How are you feeling?
How are you managing?
What is challenging for you?

My feelings and thoughts are overlooked.

I learn not to talk about it. I learn to figure out things on my own. I learn to undervalue my feelings about my difference. I figure out how to be seen as "normal" pretty quickly. I am expected to be the well-behaved, "good" child with my difference unnoticeable. And though other kids see my hand during my childhood, no one really says anything about it. I make friends easily; everyone accepts me for me. Only one time in first grade do I tell my parents about a girl saying something mean about my hand; otherwise, no one ever talks about it with me.

In my teen years, I start hiding it. And, possibly to alleviate my parents' discomfort and mine, they take me to get fitted for a cosmetic prosthesis, hoping that I will stop hiding my hand. That intervention ends up not working out; I don't like the feeling of having something that, to me, feels even more uncomfortable and noticeable. The rare conversations with them about my difference aren't open; instead, they are stressful and tinged with the guilt of what they believe they must have done wrong during pregnancy and throughout most of my life.

One time, during my teenage years, my mom and I are out walking together, talking, and taking pictures in a garden; the mood is light and playful. I am swinging my arms, and the camera I am holding accidentally hits her left hand. Suddenly, everything changes.

She complains loudly, "Oh my goodness, my hand hurts so much. I can't believe this. I can't believe this. Did you do that on purpose? Now, I am going to have a huge bruise. I can't believe this."

I am shocked at the accusation and how quickly the situation has changed.

"Well, at least you have a hand, so stop complaining," I blurt out.

These are risky words. I can't believe I've said them out loud.

She immediately responds, "I knew that you have always been angry with me for your hand. I am so sorry I caused this."

"I'm not angry with you; it's just that you're making a big deal about a bruise on your hand that will disappear. My hand will never grow."

And with that, the conversation ends.

Insight: When we "refuse to see" difference, we may mistakenly silence or alienate those we intend to support.

I find that bringing up my hand is something that brings her tremendous shame. As a child, I learn that she will cry and blame herself when I bring it up.

Like many parents, my mom and dad don't know how to bring up this tough conversation; it's not easy, and they have no support or role models to lean on. I never share my musings with my parents about how I wonder what my life would be like if I had been born with two hands. I fantasize about how much better and easier it would be. I imagine I would be more successful. That I would find love more easily. That I wouldn't struggle. Everything would fall into place if I just had my left hand. I come to believe that I have to wrestle with my difference on my own.

Reflection Questions

Think about your childhood.

What was talked about in your household? What was not?

What do you wish your family had known about you growing up?

2

ON BEING DIFFERENT

Noticing I am different.
Finding ways to fit in.

In this chapter:

New situations can bring to light differences about yourself that you may not have been aware of previously. I share how starting at a new school created so much discomfort that I compulsively started to hide my hand, never imagining the hiding would last beyond a particular day, let alone the many years to come.

The Discovery

Why must I leave my old school? I am comfortable here. I have good friends, and I am popular. I know what the teachers want each year, and I am the teachers' pet. Now, I face learning everything new: a new route to school, a new building, new teachers, and making all new friends.

I am ten years old.

My parents are focused on my education and decide to transfer me to a private girls' school in the middle of fifth grade. Switching schools in the middle of the year is never easy because you're usually the only new student. Everyone already seems to have best friends, and people wonder why I've transferred now—something must be wrong with me.

It's the first week in my new school. I sit by myself, away from the other girls, in the gymnasium turned auditorium, waiting for drama auditions to start. I am excited about being on stage—I like performing and feel like this is a way to make friends. I wear a school uniform for the first time: it's a green tartan skirt, a crisp, white Peter Pan-collar blouse, a navy-blue sweater, and blue knee-high wool socks with penny loafers. My hair is the Dorothy Hamill-style haircut—the definitive look for girls in the late 1970s.

Off to my left, I notice a group of four older girls staring at me.

Confused, I think they can't be staring at me.

I am nobody; I am new. Maybe that's why they are looking at me?

Then, I notice that it's not me they are staring at; it is my hand. And I hear them whispering to one another, "Is she the new girl? Why is she here? What do you think happened to her hand?"

My face turns hot.
I don't understand why these girls are looking at my hand so intently.

In my other school, the kids already knew about my hand and didn't make it a big deal.

I feel self-conscious for the first time. Aware that something is different.

I want to hide. I want to hide my hand; I force my sweater sleeve to cover it.

I immediately feel alone. I have no friends to protect me. No teachers who know me.

I am on my own.

"Hey, what happened to your hand?" one of the older girls comes over and asks bluntly.

"Nothing." I deny it. No one has ever asked me that so directly before. My sweater sleeves stretch even further over both of my hands as I nervously play with them.

The teacher calls for attention, and the play auditions begin.

The girls move away to other seats and leave me alone.

Phew, thank goodness. I exhale, relieved to dodge the inquisition.

A few days later, the same older girl approaches me; she immediately tells me she wants to be my mentor, big sister.

I feel relief. I say thank you. I nervously tell her about my hand. I've never had to do that before.

"Yeah, we already knew," she says. "We liked you anyway."

Insight: New situations can make us
see our differences in a new light.

I didn't actually remember this scene until I went to regression therapy one summer when I was 50 years old.

I thought I started really worrying about being different when I was 13, but it turns out I was actually much younger. It took regression therapy to uncover that trauma that began my hiding.

That therapist brought me into a light trance, a mental focus replaying me as a young child. As we got deeper into my memory, I remembered the gymnasium incident I had blocked for years.

I could picture that little Ruthie, alone and afraid, not understanding the stares, and feeling different from everyone else. Over the years, I developed a pattern of hiding, and only now do I understand the connection between starting something new and needing to hide my hand until people get to know me.

As psychologist Abraham Maslow describes in his theory on our hierarchy of needs, one's need to feel safe is critical. I remember how changing schools significantly impacted how I saw myself; it was a jolt to my comfort. I began to feel very unsafe.

Some of the most "normal" changes can cause disruption, such as starting a new school, moving, or changing jobs. We don't always understand their effect in the moment, but even a slight shift can be monumental. That change can also allow people to know us in a different context. We get to reintroduce ourselves and hope people accept us; often, we only reveal what we want others to see.

Reflection Questions

Thinking through your life, when have you felt different?

When did you first truly notice you were different?
Were you made aware of your gender in a new context?
Your skin color? Ethnicity? Religion? Body type?

What external messages have you heard about your difference?

3

TAUGHT TO HIDE

Learning to hide.

Of course, I hid.
I incorporated messages about the stigma of difference into
how I saw myself.
For so many of us, there are external cues that we internalize.
We turn to hiding.
Many of us are hiding parts of ourselves.

In this chapter:

I explore why many of us hide parts of ourselves and don't feel like we fit in. We hold incredible shame and picture those parts of ourselves as so much worse than they actually are; we convince ourselves we won't be accepted if we reveal ourselves fully. Often, the self-perception is that you are the only one with a difference. You have normalized the hiding so much that you don't even recognize it as hiding until you start to explore those areas of your life.

Me, Hiding

I am a child, carefree and unafraid.

I first feel different when I start a new school in fifth grade, but now that I'm a teenager, the feeling intensifies as I begin high school. Almost overnight, my world changes. I feel different. I want to fit in.

I hold a big secret from everyone.

Insight: Your differences can make
you feel alone, afraid, and unlovable.
We hide the most beautiful and
unique parts of ourselves
just to fit in.

I become obsessed with hiding my hand, a part of myself that I find ugly and unsightly. I hide it for years.

I don't think anyone will understand. I feel alone and embarrassed. I live in fear.
Afraid of what others might think about me when they find out.
Afraid of how they judge me.
Afraid no one will want to date me because they find me unattractive.

I am alone and disconnected.
I worry and constantly forecast my next steps so that my hand won't be discovered.
My anxiety takes over, so I cancel plans.
I stop living my life.

I don't know how to self-soothe and dismiss the negative thoughts.
I feel trapped in my head, unsure how to free myself.
I am envious of others and their carefree lives.

I don't share my thoughts and feelings with anyone.
I convince myself I am alone, unattractive, and unlovable.

I am a young girl negotiating the world of difference by myself.

Being Taught

Taught to Hide, Learning to Unhide is the first working subtitle of this book, *Singlehandedly*—my dad immediately objects to the word "taught."

"We didn't teach you to hide. That implies it was something we showed you how to do," he says adamantly.

"Actually, you did. Not as a directive but through your influence. Mom hid behind her need to look perfect, and you hid through your need to fit into a different culture. You both were my first role models of hiding."

He doesn't totally buy my argument.

My mom was extraordinarily beautiful, to the point that people would often stop her when we were walking anywhere and ask if she was a model or an actress. She wasn't. She was just my mom.

She never let anyone see her without makeup, including my dad. She would wake up extra early every morning to start her makeup ritual, sit in front of a round mirror, and paint her skin with beautiful jars of expensive, high-end makeup—Chanel, Borghese. She reperformed that routine each night before my dad got home from work. My mom never wanted my dad—or anyone—to see her as imperfect. Though he never asked her to make herself up for him, she did it because that was her way of protecting herself, and it was what she was taught good wives do.

Covering her face with makeup was her way of feeling attractive and fighting her insecurities about her own beauty. Like many women, she used makeup to make herself desirable; she used it to fit society's beauty standards. My mom also used makeup to fight her more personal demons, which came from her own mother, who was overly critical of my mom's looks during her childhood. She came from an alcoholic family that overvalued beauty. She naturally adopted the role of the "looking-good" child, so all would be "perfect" on the outside, despite the turmoil at home.

My mom also hid behind oversized sunglasses; she wore them everywhere. Outdoors, of course, and always indoors, too—in airports, theaters, and restaurants. Her mother had told her early on that her eyes were too small and unattractive; sunglasses and makeup were her way of hiding those things she determined were her "non-beauty," a way to protect herself from the world. She hid.

My dad also hid. From what I observed, he hid his cultural Judaism, dated non-Jewish women, and eventually married my mom, an Episcopalian. My parents even moved to a very WASP, non-Jewish town in Connecticut. He didn't join a local synagogue, didn't insist that his children be raised Jewish or that his wife convert. We did not celebrate any Jewish holidays. Even the people in his family who were considered beautiful didn't "look Jewish." At restaurants when making reservations, we changed our last name from Rathblott to Reed, which he now claims was just for the ease of making a reservation. I always understood it as a way to hide our Jewish last name and avoid dealing with anti-Semitism.

These were the impressions and deductions I made as a child. I learned early on that you had to hide certain aspects of yourself to be accepted and fit in. Hiding became a way to self-protect.

Insight: Hiding is a way of
protecting yourself and making
others comfortable.

We learn messages about difference and acceptance from a very young age. We understand that one way to protect ourselves and fit in is to hide those parts of ourselves that are considered "different."

They say you get your first social cues from your family. Though it may seem trivial and not explicit, these little nuances significantly impacted my identity. I learned that you hide the parts of yourself that you find unattractive or undesirable. You conceal your blemishes behind makeup. You hide from the world behind sunglasses. You hide your religion to avoid negative community sentiments.

My dad is correct. The directive wasn't explicit; it was implicit. I picked up on the social cues and clues by watching their behavior. I imitated them.

The White Glove

I am 11 years old.

In my hometown, we have a dance school led by an old-school professional dancer. He's legendary and very formal. He expects perfection. For him, dance instruction is not only a tool to teach dance; it's a method to instill the strong character traits of timeliness, respect, and confidence in young people. Girls are required to wear dresses and white gloves while boys dress in suits with ties. Boys ask girls to dance, except for the occasional change-up nights when the roles reverse.

My mom signs me up for classes. She keeps telling me, "I wish my parents had *cared* this much about me and provided me with the same opportunities."

I am not excited. I don't understand why I have to attend mandatory weeknight rehearsals and wear the white gloves when no one else in my new school is going.

And, I wonder, *how on earth will I wear the white glove with only one hand? It seems impossible.*

My mom thinks of a solution. "I know; we will stuff the white glove with tissue to make it look like fingers."

"But how will it stay on?"

"We will secure it to your wrist with rubber bands."

Hmmm, I think. *Will it work? Can I pull it off?*
Can I really fool people, especially boys, into thinking I can wear two gloves?
Can I make it work?

The rubber band is wrapped super tight around the white glove so as not to slip off my wrist. The constriction hurts immensely, and it cuts off some of my circulation. I notice my little hand turns a whitish color when I remove the glove.

I am willing to deal with the pain if it means I can look normal.

During the first dance, I immediately worry the glove is going to come off. I imagine that the fake glove goes flying with just one random swing movement or while my partner is holding it.

How will I handle that humiliation?

But luckily, it stays on. Success. Phew.

But, I hate the white gloves.

Week after week, I feel sick. Waves of anxiety pulsate through me. I wonder, *Will this be the week the glove falls off?* After every class, I breathe a sigh of relief and beg not to have to return.

I hate the uncertainty of being out of control; it is too much.

The white gloves symbolize shame; they are a disownment of who I am, making me feel like I am pretending.

I am literally stuffing a part of myself to fit in. I hate the discomfort and deceit.

Luckily, there are always two boys whom I can count on to dance with me. They know about my hand and quell some of my anxiety. I feel safe that they know.

Insight: By hiding part of ourselves
to fit in, we create a façade of
perfection.

This was the first time I had to hide my hand from others; it was expected.

I learned that to be accepted by others, I had to find ways to look like everyone else.

It reinforced that my feelings weren't important and that fitting in was. I learned that my emotions were being stuffed away too. I wasn't being heard when I complained about the anxiety, so I learned to suppress it and not share it. I wasn't asked how I felt but instead received the message it was better just to comply. I learned not to question the covering.

As I look back, I wonder what the alternative would have been. Did my parents ever try to talk to the instructor about options for the white glove? Or were they so caught up in the prestige of being part of this activity that they didn't think of advocating for me for fear of upsetting his rules? Did compliance prove that I could be accepted? Did it confirm that they could be accepted?

My body was different and less than *perfect*, but I could fool people into believing I was *whole* when I hid.

In My Pocket

I am 13 years old.

Climbing up the steps of the yellow school bus on the first day of school, I sit in the front row, right behind the driver. My house is one of the first stops on the route. I am starting at a new coed high school.

As more and more kids get on the bus, I get nervous. I see all these new faces, potentially new friends, and I just want to be liked. I look down. My little hand seems different and out of place. It feels weird, and just like with the girls in middle school, I feel like everyone is going to look at it. I don't feel like I fit in. I worry that someone is going to notice and ask me about it. I just want to look like everyone else.

I impulsively tuck my little hand into the front left pocket of my tight blue jeans.

I don't have long sleeves because it is still warm weather; hiding it in my front pocket feels safe—like it won't be noticed.

I think: *I am just hiding it for the bus ride, just until I get to school.*

I extend the time: *This is just to get me through the first day.*

Just when I am walking in the hallways.

Just in certain classes.

My list of places and times for hiding my hand keeps growing. I hide it more and more. I don't know how to stop.

I expand my hiding by wearing sweaters with extra-long sleeves, holding my backpack in front of me with my hand tucked under it, carrying my textbooks and notebooks with my hand sandwiched between them, heading to my locker before class is dismissed so the hallways will be empty. I make my hand invisible so no one will notice me.

I just want to fit in. I want two hands.

Everyone else in my classes looks so confident; they are smiling and free. They are getting involved in activities; they are making friends. I am hiding.

I feel ugly and awkward; I am no longer outgoing like I was in elementary and middle school. Now, I am shy and fly under the radar, rarely participating in class. I don't want to be seen as special. I stop doing the things I love. No more holding positions in student government; no more trying out for plays; no more participating in sports. The risk of being seen is too great. I sit on the sidelines instead. I blend in.

I learn to juggle so many things with one hand. Unlocking my locker while carrying an armful of books, balancing a tray filled with food and a drink and weaving through a crowded cafeteria as I search for an empty seat, changing in gym class using only one hand—buttoning my shirts, zipping my pants, tying my shoes.

I am getting really good at using only one hand while perfecting hiding the other. I become more and more fearful that if someone sees my hand, I will be ostracized from everything.

I bury myself further and further in secrecy.

Insight: Hiding can become an obsession that impacts all areas of your life.

I had no idea that that one decision on the bus would affect me for the next 25 years.

As psychologist Erik Erikson talks about in his theory of psychosocial development, adolescence is a stage of separating or individuating ourselves from our parents and fitting in with our peers. It was a stage of healthy development: my peers noticed me, and I just wanted to fit in.

I was petrified of rejection, so I hid my hand to protect myself.

I was worried someone would say my hand was "gross." I saw it as deformed and was worried everyone else would, too. In truth, hiding became just as much about protecting me as it was about protecting others from having to see "my deformity."

When I was hiding, all I saw were my differences. I saw other teenagers with two hands, and I didn't see anyone who looked like me. I didn't see anyone struggling; it appeared everyone else's life was easy. I wanted my body to be "normal," like everyone else's. I tried to fit in by hiding the part of me that was different.

I came to believe that people would like me if I looked like everyone else.

Hiding was my ticket to acceptance and fitting in, even if that meant giving up what I enjoyed.

The Prosthesis

"Why don't you just get a prosthesis?"

Many people have asked me this over the years. In asking this question, they generally make two assumptions:

One, that I have never considered it or never had a prosthesis.

Two, that it would be better than the way I was hiding my hand.

I made two attempts at using a prosthesis.

Attempt one. I am six months old.

The doctors recommend to my parents that I get a prosthesis to help me crawl because they worry that I won't develop normally if I don't develop the arm strength to pull myself up on my left side. So, like any "good parents" who believe doctors must know best, my mom and dad have me fitted for one.

They place the hard plastic sleeve over my little hand; I try to crawl. It's a disaster.
I keep hitting my head with the rigid plastic, causing black and blue facial bruises every time I try to move forward.

Trusting their intuition and advocating for what is best for me, my parents remove the prosthetic after a week.

I figure out how to crawl perfectly well on my own and build strength in my arm.

Attempt two. I am 16 years old.

My parents notice I am hiding more and more. I am even beginning to slouch my shoulders to my left side; my posture is off, not aligned. They discuss what to do in private together; I am not privy to their conversations.

They hear about a company that makes perfect replica cosmetic prostheses. The cost is about $10,000. Luckily, my dad has good insurance and the assistance of internal human resources to help navigate the bureaucracy, so the cost is covered.

This is one of the first times my parents give attention to my hand. I am not sure what to think. My mom takes me to get fitted for the prosthesis. We walk in and are ushered back to a private room and meet the artist who will design my hand. The artist studies every detail of my right hand to match it perfectly to create a "new" left hand. I go for at least two design fittings.

I am quite uncomfortable: not because of the laborious process, but because my little hand is fully exposed for the first time in years. I haven't let anyone see my hand or touch it in years.

We drive back for the final fitting, the big reveal. I try on the finished product. I stare at it in the mirror.

Aghast. Speechless.

I can't believe how real it looks.
I think to myself, *So, this is what it is like to have two hands.*
It is strange and surreal. I keep staring. I never imagined it.
I am hopeful for freedom from hiding. It feels strange.

I wear a bracelet on my wrist to cover where the prosthesis ends and where my actual skin starts, so no one can tell. There are no hooks or ties to hold the prosthesis in place; this new faux hand simply relies on the tight fit at the wrist.

The more I wear it, the more I notice that the prosthesis feels heavy and weighs down my wrist.
It has a rubbery smell.
It gets super hot inside and sweaty; it smells like sweaty socks when I remove it.

But I try to like it because I want the illusion of having two hands. This is the start of my new life.

I show up at school wearing the hand. I haven't told any of my friends about it. And I hope they will just see me as "normal" now. I confidently walk up to a group of girls.

Immediately, one of the girls points and shouts, "Oh my god, what happened to your hand? What is that? It looks fake and weird."

Others nod in agreement with her.

I am crushed, beyond crushed. My hopes for "normal" are dashed within seconds.

Her words are cruel, but I decide I actually like the way it looks. Instead of caving to peer pressure, I want to see if people who don't know me will think it's real. I find the nerve to give it a try in a social setting with boys; I wear it to a school dance.

Immediately, a boy asks me to dance; I say yes.

As we start to move, rather than feeling confident and two-handed, I keep worrying about this thing attached to me falling off and being discovered. This would be the worst possible outcome.

It reminds me of the white glove.

I determine that wearing this thing is so much worse than just hiding my hand. There's an added layer of uncertainty. I can't predict or control what will happen when it's in someone else's hand. I wear it until the end of the dance and then remove it immediately.

I decide never to wear it again. I go back to my tried and trusted way; my hand goes back in my pocket. I conclude that, at least when I hide it, I am in control.

Years later, I find the prosthesis tucked away in a brown cardboard box on a shelf in our freezer, kept there to preserve it, just in case I ever want to try again. I never do.

Insight: Sometimes, we substitute
one way of hiding for another,
thinking it will be better. It's
often not.

The prosthesis was supposed to make me look "perfect," based on traditional beauty norms, and yet, I didn't feel perfect at all. I felt ashamed that my hand was hideous. I had to cover my hand to look perfect, so that I could convince myself and others that I had two hands. The message I heard with the prosthesis was that it was better to hide your hand rather than be seen as imperfect.

As I think back, I just couldn't deal with the idea of having a "fake" hand. I realize this sounds contradictory because I was "faking it" by hiding my little hand in other ways. For me, wearing a prosthesis seemed like adding another unnecessary layer to my hiding. I preferred my original method.

While hiding was definitely a weight that held me back and made me feel disconnected from people, it also served a purpose. Hiding became my saving grace. When I hid, I felt safe, protected, and comfortable. Hiding allowed me to live in denial; I could pretend there was nothing wrong. I didn't have to face the problem if you couldn't see my little hand. I didn't have to answer questions about my hand, no one stared, there was no judgment, and I wasn't rejected because of my missing hand.

Hiding became my norm and provided a solution at a critical time in my life; I could just be like everybody else. Hiding relieved me. When I hid, I could be seen as "normal." When I hid, the monster went away; the damaged person went away. And, as I think about it, my hiding also made others comfortable; no one had to worry about saying the wrong thing, not knowing what to say, or staring too long. Hiding allowed people to see me, not my difference. It allowed me to be a blank slate. Hiding allowed me to fit in and not even think about being different.

Hiding became my friend.

Even the Most Popular Girl

Over the years, I reconnect on social media with many of my former classmates, including the most popular girl in our high school class. She and I happen to find ourselves in the same city, and we meet for lunch.

I am 49 years old.

As we are catching up and reliving high school memories, I open up to her about the isolation and loneliness that I experienced during school and how I was hiding my hand.

She immediately says that she understands. "I, too, felt really disconnected; I didn't feel like I fit in or had a real group of friends until much later in high school."

What? She always seemed to have it all together: student government, sports, dates, friends. I can't believe we shared similar teen awkwardness; I only wish I had known that back then.

Insight: We aren't alone in
discomfort, even if we think we are.
Most people don't have
it all together.

I was so worried about fitting in that I hid the part of myself that I found so uncomfortably different in high school. The more I hid my hand, the lonelier I felt. I envied my classmates whose lives looked so much easier; it appeared from the outside that they had no actual stress or anxiety outside of typical teen issues like dating, getting along with their parents, or doing well in school. Now, looking back, that assumption is preposterous. Nevertheless, I was shocked. I couldn't understand how even the most popular student could feel alone; I thought I was the only one.

We often feel as if we are the only ones struggling and that everyone else has it all together. We believe we are alone in our hiding. Yet, if we all opened up, we might find that we wrestle with similar feelings collectively. The human experience of feeling disconnected or lonely is universal.

I Didn't Think I Was Hiding

I am 52 years old.

I am thinking about a potential new target audience for my speaking, so I reconnect with a woman from my professional network who works in that area; I haven't spoken with her in several years. We schedule a call to connect.

We are about thirty minutes into our conversation when she asks, sort of out of the blue, "Were you the one who put that poll question on LinkedIn about hiding part of yourself in the workplace?"

A few months earlier, I ran a poll to survey my LinkedIn connections about whether they were hiding part of themselves to test the Deloitte study about covering because I believed that the number of people covering was higher than the 61% previously reported.

I reply, "Yes."

"Well, I automatically answered 'no,' but now, after speaking with you, I realize I have been hiding two big parts of my life."

"Interesting. How are you hiding?"

"Well, I was hired during COVID, and my coworkers only know me through Zoom calls. And even though I offer my opinion constantly and am always expressing myself, I realize no one really knows anything personal about me. I don't talk about the pain in my feet that is debilitating to the point I can't walk. No one knows. And I don't share about my child's severe mental challenges."

She pauses. "I don't want anyone to know because I worry that they will think I can't do the job physically, and they will judge me for being a bad mother and think I am not committed to the job if I have to take time off to care for my child."

I take a deep breath and say, "So many of us don't share part of ourselves for fear of judgment. You're not alone."

"But, I am worried about going into the office and having to explain my situation. You've really made me think." She exhales.

Insight: Even though hiding can feel like a good solution, it often provides a false sense of fitting in. Hiding can even *create* additional problems or obstacles.

At first, hiding seems harmless, but it slowly invades your life. Hiding becomes your life. It's a lot like lying: the more you do it, the harder it is to stop; the more you lie, the more you believe it to be the truth yourself, and the more you get away with it. Hiding inevitably leads to shame and disconnection from ourselves and others; it chips away at your self-acceptance and authentic connections with others because they aren't getting to know the real you.

I had relied on my methods of hiding and covering my hand for so many years and had given them so much power. I rationalized that I could be seen as beautiful if no one saw my hand. It was as if I were living as two different people: one with a hideous hand who would never be considered beautiful, who would never find love, who was trapped in this misery because she did not have a full hand, and the other a con artist, accepted only because she was able to fool people into believing that she had two hands.

When we hide things about ourselves because we think they are personal flaws, we deny people the opportunity to really get to know us.

For some of us, hiding becomes so normalized that we don't even consider it to be hiding. It becomes part of who we are, and we think we are the only ones hiding. But when we peel back the layers, we find many more people are not sharing parts of themselves for fear of shame and judgment.

Often, the secrets and shame we carry become more prominent than the actual thing we are hiding.

For me, hiding became my disability, not my hand.
Hiding prevented me from living my life fully.

Reflection Questions

Have you ever hidden part of yourself for fear of not being accepted?
What do you hide?
How do you hide?
Where and when do you hide?
Why do you hide?

How is hiding holding you back from being the best version of yourself?

4

AWKWARD MOMENTS

Living with difference isn't always easy.

We internalize the negative messages we receive from the world about difference and believe them to be true.

In this chapter:

Awkward moments can arise as a result of hiding. You hide because you fear judgment and often hold paralyzing shame. You picture those parts of yourself as so much worse than they actually are and convince yourself that you won't be accepted if you reveal yourself fully. A natural response to feeling different is the desire to look and act like everyone else. However, when you try to fit in, you make your differences appear easily overcome to others, and you reduce their discomfort while increasing your own. By covering up your challenges, you don't genuinely provide others an opportunity to get to know you.

You Don't Have to Touch It

I am 18 years old.

Walking home after a college party, my best friend and I decide to find our way back to our dorm by ourselves; it's later than we think, and the path back seems darker and unlit. We clutch each other nervously, making up stories of an attack; we even put our keys between our fingers, as we've been taught in self-defense. We cling to each other.

On impulse, she clutches me and grabs my little hand. I pull back and stammer, "You don't have to touch it; I know it's disgusting."

She retracts her grasp in an act of comfort to me. We don't discuss it.

Insight: The distorted image we
build in our minds about our
difference is so much worse than
the reality of the thing itself.

Even as I write this now and say it aloud, I tear up.

How could I have thought so little of myself? How could I have formed such an awful self-image and felt so worthless?

That young woman, beautiful in so many ways, thought so little of herself. She felt ugly. She felt damaged. She felt inadequate. She couldn't even let her best friend innocently touch her hand. Come to think of it, I had never let *anyone* touch it. I don't remember my parents ever really touching it, and I am certain I had never really touched it myself.

In my late twenties, I saw a therapist to work through dating challenges. I was in the deep throes of hiding my hand; I even hid it from my therapist.

He asks to see it.

There was no way I was going to show him; I had safeguarded it for too long.

My hand is buried deep.

There's no way I can let him see it.

During one session, he says, "Describe your left hand to me and tell me why it would be so bad to show it."

"There is no way you want to see it; it's monstrous, deformed, ugly, and scary."

I can barely look at him. I am filled with shame. My hand is so awful.

"It's worse than Frankenstein," I tell him.

I fear that even he, a therapist, will be scared. I can't handle his reaction.

He's persistent in bringing it up during each session.
It takes weeks to build up the courage to show him.
I lose sleep many nights before our appointments because of my anxiety.

I feel disfigured. I don't want to look at my hand; why would any-one else?

After several more weeks, I muster the courage and strength to show him; it is just a quick glimpse at the end of the session on my way out the door.

I am relieved; he doesn't scream in horror. He simply says, "Okay, thank you."

I go back to hiding, but the door of truth has been opened just a little.

Only years later, I realize that my mental image of my hand and the messages I had internalized were distorted and didn't match reality.

A Single Ski Pole

I am in middle school.

We take a family ski trip. Like most beginners, I learn how to ski without poles on the bunny hill. Eventually, I graduate to needing poles, but I quickly realize that I don't need both. I feel more balanced just using one.

When I rent my skis, though, they won't let me rent just one pole; the sticks come in pairs. I must take both, which means I have to find a ski rack to lock up the unused pole while I am out skiing. At the end of the long ski day, I search for what feels like an eternity to find that secured pole; otherwise, I face a penalty fee for a "lost pole."

While I wait in line for the chair lift on the slopes, almost every ski lift operator notices my one pole and shouts to me, "Hey, did you lose your pole?"

At first, I am honest and explain, "I only need one because I only have one hand."

This makes me feel embarrassed in front of the waiting line of people, and the operator truthfully doesn't know what to say in response; he's in shock.

Eventually, I come up with the excuse "I broke my arm," thinking that sounds plausible, but I find that causes even more unneeded conversation and attention.

Finally, I agree and say, "Yeah, I dropped it off the chairlift."

With that, most operators seem satisfied and helpfully refer me back to rentals. I nod and move on.

Insight: It can feel easier to lie than to
explain a situation when you are hiding.
But every lie adds to the burden of the
illusion you are upholding and chips
away at your self-acceptance.

I learn that lying is sometimes the easiest way to hide. Lying prevents you from drawing attention to a situation and can make others feel comfortable. It's just easier.

One-Handed Glove

I am in my thirties.

A friend gave me a pair of gloves one year for the holidays. Innocent enough.

Gloves have fingers. I am reminded of the white gloves from my youth.

I am confused.

"Gloves?" I ask with a semi-sarcastic tone.

"Oh shoot, I completely forgot. Sometimes, I forget about your little hand," she admits.

I immediately create my defensive internal dialogue.

Forget? How could you forget?

I realize she doesn't forget intentionally; I just don't get that luxury of forgetting because my hand is with me every day. I am constantly reminded about my missing hand and all the toxic messages I hold about it.

She offers, "Well, maybe you can just use one of them?"

"That seems weird," I say, "I don't think I can pull off Michael Jackson's one-glove style."

She shrugs.

I place the gloves on a shelf and never use them.

Insight: Sometimes, we forget about others' differences because it's not how we see them—it's not their whole self.

People often say things to me like, "I don't even see you as different," or, "I never think about your hand." These aren't meant to be mean-spirited. Rather, I realize that I make it easy for people to forget because I don't talk about my hand. By not sharing my stories of difference and challenge, I make it easy for people to forget and not to acknowledge them.

Making It Easy for Others

As someone born with a limb difference, I spend much of my life learning to accommodate and accomplish things in ways that people can't even imagine. And while I make daily activities that most people do with two hands look effortless, it's not always easy. Just a few examples of things I do with one hand include:

- Clasping necklaces
- Putting backings on earrings
- Blow drying my hair
- Buttoning shirts

- Zipping jackets
- Changing the sheets on the bed
- Typing emails and texting
- Cooking breakfast, buttering toast
- Cutting food with a knife
- Grocery shopping and then carrying all the bags
- Holding an umbrella and talking on a cellphone at the same time

I pride myself on not asking for help. I have spent a lifetime figuring out challenges and learning to overachieve.

Insight: When we rely on ourselves
for solutions, we often feel we
can't ask for help. When we hide,
we don't know how to ask for our
needs to be met. We also don't
become important to ourselves.

As a child, I figured things out. I became super independent; no one had to worry about me. For so many years, I made it easy for people to forget that I had only one hand. I even doubled up on challenging tasks; I rarely made more than one trip carrying grocery bags home. I always carried all the luggage on trips. I did it to prove that I was self-sufficient, even with just one hand.

I rarely talked about my emotional discomfort. There was also physical discomfort; my hand got hot and sweaty in my pocket and under long-sleeved sweaters.

I learned that it made things much easier for everyone when I hid or felt like it did. When I was hiding, people didn't have to deal with their discomfort around disability by looking away or wavering on what to say. I allowed others to stay comfortable.

I always worried and was constantly anticipating my next steps: I didn't order things that were hard to cut in a restaurant; I made sure all of my outfits, even dresses, always had pockets; I thought about who I was sitting next to just in case a situation arose where we had to hold hands. I rarely relaxed unless I was home alone in my own space. In college, I even advocated for a single room without roommates each year so that I would have a space to unhide.

I feared being a burden that someone would have to do something for me. I spent a lot of time proving my independence.

As someone born with a disability, I spent years fighting to be seen as capable, looking for solutions, thinking outside the box, and forecasting my next steps. I avoided drawing attention to my disability by making it look easy to manage. I anticipated solutions to problems before they arose, such as learning how to be confident at a cocktail party, balancing a drink and food, greeting people, and shaking hands. I hoped that others wouldn't notice.

I learned how to be seen as able and capable, successful. I learned to be "extra" intelligent, clever, and persistent.

The sacrifices I made downplayed my feelings and struggles.

I never fully grieved or tapped into feelings of sadness. I never allowed myself to get angry about being born with one hand.

I never let anyone in to know more.

Reflection Questions

Has someone shared something private with you?
How did you feel when you learned their secret?
How did you react?
Is there anything you wish you had told them? How did you follow up with them?

When have you lied about something because it seemed easier than telling the truth?

5

ASSUMPTIONS WE MAKE

Many of us make assumptions about difference.
We forget to be curious and ask questions:
About ability.
About accommodation.
About access.

We forget to express humanity and kindness.

In this chapter:

We often forget to slow down and employ curiosity when it comes to creating space for conversation about difference, which can lead to assumptions being made, particularly about someone's ability. As a result, people living with certain kinds of difference are often pushed to continue hiding or prove their ability. It's important to ask people how we can support them and push past our own discomfort and biases.

Can You Do It?

I am 20 years old.

My dad encourages me to send my resume and cover letter to several law firms where he has contacts. Only one sends a response back. I attend an interview. I land a coveted summer internship at a New York City law firm. It's an incredible paid opportunity, and I get to take the train and commute to the city every day. It feels very adult.

My job that summer is to put together a presentation on why a specific box top deserves a patent. It requires cutting out copies of products made by similar competitors and stitching them into a report. I am thrilled to have my own project, something to use to prove my competence. I am very achievement-focused and like to be in charge.

In the office, all the summer interns and paralegals sit at a long table built into the floor, our chairs closely spaced next to one another. We look out large glass windows facing downtown, with amazing views of skyscrapers; it's the ultimate New York City panorama. I can see the Empire State Building and the Twin Towers. It's like a scene from a postcard.

These are the days before computers, cell phones, or the internet, so there are no distractions, instead just huge law books to review to pass the time; we all work diligently and track our work activities with hourly journal entries. I am relieved to have my project to fill my day.

On my first day, I show up at the office promising myself that I will try not to hide my hand in this new situation. However, I quickly regress into my old routine even as I am riding up in the elevator. My hand ends up back in my pocket.

About three weeks into the job, the senior partner on the case calls me into his office. I am nervous and excited because someone senior is paying attention to my work.

He doesn't ask me to sit; that's not a good sign.

I stand nervously in the doorway, barely making my way into his office. His tone and demeanor seem pretty serious. He is studying the latest iteration of my project on his desk.

Suddenly, I feel like I am in the principal's office; I have a wave of panic, but I'm not sure what I have done wrong.

"Ruth, did you ever go to kindergarten?" he barks at me.

My mind rattles. *Yes, of course, I did.* But I can barely utter a sound.

"Because if you had, you would have learned how to use scissors!"

I look at my work sitting on his desk; I see it in a new light. It looks sloppy and unprofessional, a lot like a kindergartener's.

I have been hiding my hand, using only one hand to cut copies for the presentation display. Every time I cut, the paper slides, creating jagged, uneven edges. It's a mess.

I leave his office embarrassed and ashamed.

There is no follow-up conversation, just an unspoken understanding that my work had better improve.

I think, *This might be hopeless. This once-promising project is now a mountain of a challenge. I wonder how I can even succeed. Will I have to quit before the summer is over? Should I take the work home with me?*

Possible solutions churn in my mind. I have to find a creative, secretive way to get my work done while still hiding the part of myself I don't want to share with my coworkers.

Two things make it challenging: the summer heat and the office layout.

The warm weather makes it difficult to wear long sweaters, but, like some other staff, I claim the office is too cold, so I need a sweater or a jacket. That does the trick.

The layout of the office proves more challenging to work around. The side-by-side seating layout makes it hard to hide, and that is uncomfortable. All it takes is one sideways glance, and someone may wonder why my hand is always in my pocket. I start by hiding my hand under the law books, hoping no one will notice. It works okay, but it's not foolproof. I need a more secure and secluded place. I venture out and find empty conference rooms. I ask the front desk if I can book them because I need to spread out my work, but they are not always available.

Hmmm.

I get sent down to retrieve files in the basement. It's a damp, dark area filled with stacks of paper files. No one is around, and no one ever really goes down there. I discover my perfect hiding place.

Hallelujah.

I work out of available conference rooms during the daytime, using huge law books to hold down the paper and cut cleaner edges. When the rooms aren't available, I hide out in the basement, where I go undiscovered and can use both of my hands.

I start noticing the other interns and paralegals leave around 5 p.m. I begin staying late to get my work done with the office empty. My work improves, and the partners notice. I finish the internship.

While I figure out how to complete the job, all the sneaking around and looking for places to hide causes me to miss out on bonding with the other interns. They often have lunch together and go out after work for happy hour, while I make excuses and skip out on the excursions and connections. I feel alone. I am exhausted.

Insight: Hiding is exhausting and lonely—you have to keep up the lie and constantly worry about being discovered, and it creates disconnection from others.

While hiding forced me to be creative and think outside the box for solutions, it also limited my connection with others.

As managers, we often make assumptions about what's going on with people. We focus on performance and productivity, and we forget about people. I often wonder what it would have been like if that manager had been curious about my situation rather than merely my work output. What if he had asked instead: "Ruth, what's going on? I'm concerned about your work, as it doesn't seem at the level you can do." Or even better, "How can I support you?" I wish he had created space for me to come back and share my challenge with him. I needed to feel safe to be able to share something so personal. But he never follows up, and I finished the project with success and kept my secret.

After that internship, I vowed that no matter how bad things got at another job, I would never again hide my hand in a work setting. I believed I had succeeded at this, for a time. However, I would later discover that there were other ways of hiding that weren't physical.

You Can't Sit There

I am 39 years old.

I am flying back from the Caribbean.

I check in on time at the terminal; the agent notices that I have an exit row seat on her computer screen and mentions it to me. I confirm that I paid for the upgraded seat selection. I see her look at my little hand and quickly look away; she doesn't say anything except, "We are changing your seat."

Confused, I say, "Um, but I paid for the upgrade."

"Yes, you'll have a comparable seat."

I tell her I still don't understand.

She hands me the rules placard for exit row compliance.

I review it and tell her, "Yes, I meet all the terms."

She keeps sliding the paper toward me but not saying or explaining anything.

I continue to say, "Yes, I meet all the conditions; I want to keep my exit row seat."

She hands me my boarding pass with my exit row seat, then looks away and signals for the next guest.

I am dismissed.

Relief. I have my seat, and I head to my gate.

It is not a large airport, so I don't have to walk very far to the gate. I make myself comfortable in the waiting area, and then, suddenly, I hear my name over the loudspeaker several times. It sounds urgent.

"Ruth Rathblott, come see the gate agent immediately. Ruth Rathblott, come see the gate agent immediately."

Panicked, thinking the call foreshadows terrible news, I rush to see the agent. As I wait in line, the loudspeaker blasts my name again.

"Ruth Rathblott, come see the gate agent immediately."

I tell the gate agent my name. Without explanation, she hands me a new boarding pass with a new seat assignment.

I say, "I don't understand."

Once again, I receive the exit row rules placard. She doesn't say anything.

"Yes, I have seen this already back when I checked in. I told them I can perform all the exit row duties."

She says nothing and moves on to the next passenger.

I leave her feeling embarrassed and ashamed, wishing I had worn long sleeves and hidden my hand. Maybe they wouldn't have noticed and made such presumptions about me and my abilities if I had done so. I might have been able to keep my seat.

Insight: When we don't have the courage to engage with people on a person-to-person level but instead only engage with them based on one facet of their identity, we make them feel invisible.

Often, disability is not acknowledged directly.

No one talked to me. No one would acknowledge my disability out loud. The airline staff treated me as insignificant, as though they knew my level of ability better than I did. What added insult to the situation was that, given my "disability," no one offered help with any other accommodations. No one offered to help me carry my bags up the airplane stairs or to help put them in the overhead bin.

Interestingly, this incident occurred as I was starting to unhide my hand, which only reinforced my belief that people often make baseless assumptions about disability without ever asking about a person's ability. Instead of talking to me and treating me with kindness and humanity, they kept shoving the rules' placard at me without explanation. And, when I did voice my complaint, no one heard it or took me seriously. This discrimination happens all the time to people with disabilities.

We make assumptions about ability only by what we see, and we often do so without basis. There are no strength tests for exit row seating and no way to prove that one can assist with opening the door. There is an assumption made: anyone with two hands can do it. Period. There are no actual tests to confirm you can meet exit row tasks other than a voiced "yes" when the flight attendant asks if you are willing to help. They still serve alcohol to passengers in that row, and no one checks what medications you are taking. It's common knowledge that people sit in the exit row for the extra space; it's rarely for altruistic reasons of helping in a crisis.

It seemed unfair. However, I would have been fine if the airline had administered a strength test that determined my ability to perform. But that test doesn't exist, and no one was even willing to acknowledge the discrimination. When I got home, I immediately wrote to the airline's CEO to voice my complaint and offer my suggestion for creating a test; I never heard back. I also contacted the Federal Aviation Administration (FAA) to ask why there isn't a strength test requirement. In their response, they told me not to pursue legal action because they have "lots of lawyers."

It took me a while to want to book an exit row seat again. I didn't want to suffer the embarrassment or humiliation of being refused the seat. Recently, though, I have noticed that the design of the exit row doors on certain flights has been changed, and the doors appear much easier to open, with pull-down handles. I will try my hand at an exit row again.

Update 2022: At a party, I meet a woman who used to handle airline passenger complaints. I am thrilled to have an opportunity to share my experience with an actual expert. After hearing about my automatic seat reassignment, she comments emphatically, "The airline did the right thing. They can be liable for a person with a disability sitting in an exit row seat. Imagine if there had been an accident and someone found out that someone with a disability was sitting there."

I am shocked. I tell her, "I disagree; it wasn't right."

I try to find another way to appeal to her humanity and impress upon her the unfairness of the situation. She won't listen, repeating the refrain, "They did the right thing."

When I mention how dehumanizing it was for the agent not to address me and name it as a disability issue, she again repeats, "They did the right thing."

She isn't hearing me or my frustration. By exhibiting the same disregard and insensitivity, I share that she showcases the same ableism I experienced years ago. She similarly assumes my inability without having any frame of reference for my ability, without the results of any test proving whether I can or can't perform certain duties.

I tell her, "There is no test to prove that I couldn't open the plane's exit row door. And by not acknowledging what I am saying or how I am feeling, you reinforce an ableist attitude toward those with disabilities."

I continue, "If the airline were seriously worried about liability, they wouldn't serve alcohol to passengers in those rows. They would forbid any passengers taking mind-altering medications from sitting there and even drug test people seated in the exit row. They would prioritize the passenger's age, health, and fitness level."

She stares blankly and says nothing.

"I am determined to get an exit row strength test in my lifetime," I promise her.

She wishes me good luck but repeats, "They did the right thing."

We Can't Hire Her

I am going through a stack of resumes for a front office receptionist with a colleague in my office.

"We can't hire this one," she announces.

Curious, I ask, "Why not?"

"Because when I called her for a pre-screen interview, I noticed she had a stutter."

"So?"

"Ruth, this is a front-facing position."

"So?"

"Well, we just can't have someone with a stutter at the front desk answering calls and greeting people," she says adamantly.

I review the resume again and challenge her assumption.

"This candidate has held the same position at several other companies for considerable lengths of time. Unless her resume is fabricated, it seems only fair to bring her in for an interview."

I pause and add, "I am definitely glad somebody else hired me."

She looks at me, confused.

"Because of my limb difference, you may have assumed that I couldn't do things."

A lightbulb goes off; she says she understands.

She calls the candidate to bring her in for an interview.

Insight: We often make assumptions
about people's disabilities based
on our own biases without taking
the time to properly gauge their
abilities.

When we make assumptions about a person's ability without allowing them to share their comfort with specific tasks and potential challenges, we miss out on opportunities: not only for the individual, but for the workplace itself.

You Can't Do It

I am 52 years old.

On a trip to Central America, I take a morning to try my hand at zip lining. Harnessing up, I notice I have no protective orange gloves.

I ask the guide, "Well, what about my gloves?"

He says, "Oh. You won't need them because you'll be going on the back of a buddy."

Without even referring to my hand, I know what he means.

"Absolutely not. I downhill ski, kayak, and waterski. I want the same experience as everyone else here."

He looks away. I am frustrated.

Luckily, another guide standing nearby overhears us. He interrupts and says, "You'll be fine. You only need one hand to zip line, and that's for the brake."

He hands me my orange gloves.

I zip line just fine solo.

Insight: Instead of making
assumptions about ability, ask
people what they need and how
you can support them.

The nerve of that first guide! He noticed my hand and formulated a plan based on what he imagined I could or could not do—without ever getting my input. He didn't do it to be cruel; he thought he was being helpful. In hindsight, what would have been useful is if he had given me the rules of engagement, shared what was necessary, and allowed me to decide how I could or could not participate and what support I may need. I would have been able to choose how I engaged rather than having my choice made for me or taken away entirely.

This happens all the time to people with disabilities and differences; assumptions are made about their level of ability in a particular field without ever verifying the truth. While, often, these assumptions are made with good intent, the message they send isn't always supportive, intuitive, or kind. When people avoid the topic of difference and disability because they are afraid of causing discomfort, that can perpetuate negative stereotypes and cause us to make assumptions about ability without evidence.

I can say from firsthand experience, as a person with a limb difference, that I have learned to adapt and accommodate to situations in ways that other people can't even imagine.

My advice: please stop assuming—ask instead. Ask from a place of curiosity and kindness, and ask to offer support so that someone can feel comfortable letting you know what they need.

Reflection Questions

What image is conjured in your mind when you think about:
Race? Religion? Sexuality? Gender? Weight? Eating disorders? Disability?
Chronic illness? Mental illness? Those from a different part of the country?
From different countries?

Let's take disability.
What are your immediate biases or assumptions about someone who is disabled?
How can you challenge your preconceived ideas about those with a particular disability?
How do you think about accessibility needs for those with disabilities?

Now, think about other areas of difference. Pick one from the above list.
What do you assume holds true about members of that group?
How can you challenge your preconceived notions about that group?

How do we best bring up uncomfortable topics?
What could the airline have done differently?

Mom and Dad on their wedding day

Mom and Dad bringing me home from the hospital

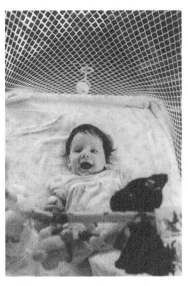

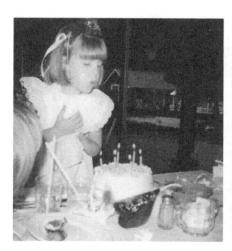 

The White Glove

One Ski Pole

Eighth Grade Graduation before I started hiding

PART TWO

FEELING EXCLUDED

6

ABLEISM

Sticks and stones...
Words can be complicated.
Sometimes, the things we say hurt more than our actions.

Our words can leave scars.

The messages we get externally can strongly influence how we
feel internally about ourselves and our differences.

In this chapter:

Ableism is discrimination based on disability. It can present as hurtful language, archaic words, and not-so-subtle messages. Ableism also shows up as hierarchy—what does and doesn't get counted as a disability. These divisive structures keep us from moving toward acceptance and advocacy. Ableism is not always intentional and can create meaningful learning opportunities and deep conversations about disability.

FREAK

I am 15 years old.

My high school report card is front and center on the kitchen table. My grades aren't good; I am underperforming academically. My mom's glowering stare makes it apparent that she is really angry.

"Do you know how important your education is?" she yells.

She is always stressing the importance of being educated; she repeatedly lectures me, especially during report card time, about how invaluable and critical it is for a woman.

"I can't believe the opportunities you are wasting. I wish I had had parents who cared this much about my education. You know, you will never be a secretary. You won't be able to type with one hand. More than anyone, YOU need an education," she continues, blasting her words close to my face.

I sit there, unable to look at her. I am in tears. I am embarrassed and ashamed.

She's never been so direct.

We've never had a conversation about my hand before. I received the message early on not to ask about it or talk about it.

She leaves the table to fetch something upstairs and orders me to wait and think about what she's said; she returns with a plain, white-covered book.

"I have been saving this book and didn't know the right time to share it with you, but since you don't take your education seriously, I need to give you a dose of reality."

FREAK.

F-R-E-A-K.

Those are the only words I see in the title of the book.

Oh, my goodness, my mom thinks I am a FREAK.

I sit in disbelief as she tries to explain the book; I drown her out as my sobbing grows louder and louder.

I can't hear anything she is saying. All I can picture are the letters F-R-E-A-K.

I leave the table and run to my bedroom, crying hysterically.

My mom thinks I am a freak.

This message isn't just coming from the outside world; it's coming from my *home*.

Insight: When we bring up difficult
subjects, we need to be mindful
and kind, creating a safe place
for discussion.

It's no wonder I hid. My mom worried that my hand would limit my success. She tried to motivate me to study and succeed by pointing out my challenges and obstacles. Unfortunately, what I heard was not a rally for success but rather a reinforcement that my hand was freakish and scary. It wasn't beautiful. It couldn't be celebrated. It would limit me.

With that feedback, I dug my hand deeper into my pocket. I clung even more tightly to hiding. I tried even harder to fly under the radar. I had to protect my hand and myself.

Hiding, for me, was about protecting myself, protecting that vulnerable piece of myself so that I could drown out the distorted messages from the world about my disability.

Hiding protected me from not being judged and not having to explain my difference.

Hiding was for self-protection and self-preservation.

"Crippled and Defect"

Calling it Crippled

I am 51 years old.

I meet a blind date for a drink at a small restaurant in New York City; he's cute and seems smart as we exchange the basics about our backgrounds, jobs, and what brings us to dating. Then we start sharing "worst date" stories, a favorite pastime of mine during dates.

"Get this, the woman was crippled," he says.

Shocked, I blurt out, "Wait, what? What do you mean? Do we even use that word anymore?"

"I showed up on the date, and she couldn't walk. She lied in her profile and photos."

Hmmm. I take an intentional pause. I am in shock and can't believe he's telling me this anecdote. My left hand is under my napkin, out of sight.

"Well, I am curious. Would you have gone out with her if she had mentioned it?"

"Probably not. But it didn't matter. She lied."

I then ask, "Well, despite her disability, did you at least have a good time?"

He said, "Yeah. But she lied. And she was crippled."

I inhale, wondering whether this is a "teachable moment," or I should just let it go and end the date.

Usually, I would dismiss the comment and not share anything about my hand because this guy wasn't what I deemed "hand-worthy." But his comments are so outrageous about disability that I feel the need to say something so that someone else doesn't get hurt by his words in the future.

I take another deep breath.

"I know we just met, and we've discussed how I speak on the topic of expanding diversity. But I must tell you; it's a little deeper than that. I want to expand diversity to fully include visible and invisible differences."

I pause.

"See, I was born with a limb difference; I am missing my left hand."

He is in shock. He doesn't say anything to me, but he quickly asks our waiter for the check.

Now, I am the one who is more in shock. An uncomfortable silence settles between us.

I fill the awkward silence of waiting. "When I share that part of myself, I'm learning to make room for men who have questions about it because some people haven't dealt with disability before. But I have to tell you the one thing I'm not willing to do is date someone who uses such archaic words about disability or views people with disabilities as being lesser."

He nods and looks away.

We leave the restaurant and awkwardly go our separate ways with a lukewarm "nice to meet you" platitude.

I wait 24 hours for him to apologize via text; he doesn't.

I delete his number.

Naming it a Defect

I am 51 years old.

I am at a wellness visit with a new doctor. As we go through my medical history, I share information about my limb difference.

"How do I code your hand?"

He sits staring at the computer screen, barely making eye contact with me.

He scrolls the list on the monitor to find the appropriate category to code my left hand.

"I don't see any field labeled limb difference. Could it be called anything else?" he asks.

"Well, the medical term I know is amniotic band syndrome," I say.

He searches. "Nope, no records for that. I see upper limb amputation, though; what about that?"

"No. I was born this way. My hand wasn't amputated. But, I remember during my childhood, they referred to it as a 'congenital birth defect,' but no one has said that in years."

He searches. Bingo. Birth defect shows up. He hits the field to save.

"Defect" is still my label.

Insight: Language about disability
still contributes to the phenomenon
of "othering"—and can make us
feel as if we are flawed or inferior.

We haven't come that far in how we think about disability; many still see it as disfiguring, debilitating, and demeaning, whether in social, work, or medical situations. Interestingly, we still categorize, code, and name disability as a defect or a deficit in medical contexts.

As I write this book and check my grammar through Grammarly, I note that Grammarly flags birth defects. It suggests that "birth defect" may be considered outdated, disrespectful, or offensive and asks me to consider changing the word or phrase to congenital disability. How come an online tool can stay current and recognize sensitivity, but the medical profession can't?

Show and Tell

I am 52 years old.

I am on a group Zoom call with a facilitator who asks us to introduce ourselves.

"I am Ruth Rathblott. I speak to expand the conversation on diversity to be fully inclusive from the lens of someone with a visible disability; I was born with a limb difference."

The facilitator says, "Yes, Ruth has a limb difference. Ruth, show everyone your hand because some people may not know what that means."

Hesitantly, I raise my small little hand.

I'm confused. Should I be doing this? I feel like a freak at the party, a circus act—the one-handed girl. I'm not sure why I don't just refuse. I feel like my younger self obeying when adults ask me to comply—wearing the white glove, taking the ski pole, answering the questions.

I feel torn because, while I have come so far with my unhiding, I am scared to disobey and make a spectacle by causing trouble and standing up for myself.

My choice is taken away.

Insight: Disability is not for show and tell. It is not a disabled person's duty or responsibility to serve as a reference of difference for others.

It's like when an acquaintance grabs my hand from across the table and holds it up to a stranger or a friend who wants her child to see it so he can get comfortable with differences. It becomes an exhibition.

I didn't protect my little hand growing up. I let her be gawked at in public and allowed myself to be made to feel uncomfortable. I didn't say no; I hid my hand. I didn't own that part of myself—instead, I let the message of being unacceptable reign strong.

My hand deserves better; I do, too. We both deserve for me to be able to say, "No."

My hand is not for show and tell. *Disability is not for show and tell.*

I Don't See You as Disabled

Throughout my life.

"I don't see you as disabled."

It sounds innocent enough.

Maybe even like a compliment?

I think it's meant to let someone know we aren't focused on your apparent difference and want to assure you that we don't see you "that way"—as something less than or as part of the stereotype. Perhaps it's because we don't want to label someone who doesn't match our definition of "that" group as being a part of it.

I hear that I shouldn't want to be part of "that" group because I am better than "that." And that part of my identity isn't important, because it's uncomfortable for others to consider, and it might challenge what they believe to be true about "that" group if it included me. My difference doesn't matter. My story and my struggles don't matter. My experience doesn't matter. It is another way of forcing me to hide, hold shame, and cover that part of myself by not acknowledging my difference and all that goes with it. The "compliment" is not so innocent; it's hurtful. Instead, I ask you to consider acknowledging my difference, being curious and asking how to support me, and sharing your areas of differences with me.

As I become more vocal about my limb difference, my disability, several people say to me directly, "Oh, I don't see you like that; you're not *really* disabled," as though they are doing me a favor by not including me in "that" group. It's as if they are thinking, *Your difference doesn't fit in with what we have been told about disability, so it causes dissonance and forces us to say you aren't "that."* And, if we assume the best intention, it's meant to be a compliment or a symbol of rescue. They believe they are doing you a favor—meaning you don't have to be defined by "that." Unfortunately, that's not how many of us take it; it's not how I take it anymore.

As part of the same conversation, I have been told that my disability doesn't count because I am not disabled enough.

Maybe we should start by expanding the definition of the word *disability.*

To me, disability means being part of a community, supporting and being supported in turn, rather than feeling isolated, alienated, and alone. It's my version of "The Ugly Duckling" fairytale, finding my flock of swans—*belonging, acceptance, and connection.*

To me, disability means *exhibiting strength and fortitude*, even when things are tough.

Disability means *overcoming challenges* and creatively *thinking outside the box* for solutions.

Disability means owning a piece of myself while also recognizing that it does not define me.

I do have a disability, and it took me a long time to accept that part of myself—over half my life. So, I am not insulted to be part of "that group." After spending years feeling isolated and left out, I now have a sense of belonging and a community.

I am proud of my disability. I wear my disability like a badge of honor. I own my disability. I own my difference. I am part of this diverse world, and I accept myself.

Insight: When we "other" people with stereotypes, labels, and judgment, we make people feel that their experience doesn't matter.

Just as I had to get comfortable and change the definition of disability in my head to something that has strength, ability, and voice, I ask you to help me change the language around disability.

The next time you find yourself about to say, I don't see you "that way," consider other things you might do. For instance:

- Acknowledge my difference, but don't treat me as different.
- Appreciate my lived experience and be curious about it when I share.

- Understand that I may need accommodation or support, not as a weakness, but as a strength. Also, realize that it can be challenging for me to ask for help.
- Join me in resetting the definition of disability by recognizing its strengths and realizing that disability itself is multifaceted—it can be visible and invisible.

Disabling Diversity

"You're not Helen Keller."

When she says this to me, I am shocked.

I am 52 years old. I haven't talked with this acquaintance in years, but we agree to connect after my TEDx release. She starts the conversation with this comparison.

I respond, "No, I'm not. I'm not blind, I'm not deaf, and I'm alive."

I get what she is implying, though. She doesn't consider my limb difference to be *disabled enough*.

She continues, "And, while I liked your TEDx video, you certainly have a lot of haters."

"I do?" I reply. I am curious to know who they are. I kind of revel in the fact that I am hitting a nerve.

"Yes, I shared your TEDx with my friends, and they want to know, 'Why is a white woman talking about diversity?'"

Wow, I thought. I purposely started my TEDx talk with the checklist of me being white, female, she/her/hers pronouns, and heterosexual. I even shared that, for much of my life, I didn't want to be seen as different; I strived to fit in. I've also worked in diverse communities for over 25 years.

"Race needs to be at the head of the line," she says. "Other groups should wait their turn."

There it is, what I had suspected—the hierarchy in diversity.

My immediate reaction: I want to delete her from my social media.

She's not open to hearing my message about expanding diversity.

But instead, I decide to keep the connection because it is information for me. And, as I had been taught many years ago by a friend, I remember her saying to me, "you can't change people, but you can change your reaction to them." It's a helpful reminder.

Insight: When we dismiss others'
differences as unimportant,
we don't allow them to feel
seen or heard.

As I build the conversation to expand diversity to be fully inclusive, more and more, I am met with sentiments like, "I'm not sure disability belongs in conversations of diversity; there are more pressing issues on the agenda."

I begin to realize there is an unspoken hierarchy around diversity. Some people judge differences, and depending on where you fit in, your difference may not matter to some groups.

Why do we do this to groups that have been marginalized? Why do we *other* one another?

When we use our differences to separate us, it keeps us from moving forward. It's not just about putting ourselves in others' shoes; it's about being curious, listening, and understanding their experiences and learning.

I have several thoughts:

- Is this the way others think about diversity, too?

- Do we pit groups against each other and, in turn, devalue others' experiences? Because if that's true, we will always remain disconnected and unsupportive of one another's differences and challenges; we will continue to keep siloing the discussions.

- How will we ever move forward with these conversations on diversity and inclusion if we keep thinking one group is more deserving than another?

When we don't acknowledge all differences in diversity, two things happen.

1. We don't have full conversations; we miss out on the benefits of diverse voices.
2. We don't create allyship or learning opportunities because people feel excluded.

Furthermore, how should we think about intersectionality in the conversations on diversity? We are all multi-dimensional. When you only look at one dimension of diversity, you disavow the experience someone has had, and you lose out on richness and depth in conversations.

Let's take gender, for example: when you only see me as a woman, it rejects my disability and my full experiences, my personal strengths, and the challenges I've overcome.

Insight: There is enough room in
the diversity conversation for all
voices if we work together.

Not including all groups in the conversation signals that some people should stay silent and keep hiding, reinforcing the message that our challenges aren't significant.

If you find yourself trying to decide if someone is "disabled enough" or if people with disabilities should be included in the diversity conversation, please stop and check yourself.

It's hurtful. It's repetitive shaming. It's an attempt to silence. That's ABLEISM.

Too many of us approach diversity conversations with a scarcity mindset, not one of abundance.

I am reminded of the "Parable of the Long Spoons," where a man has to choose heaven or hell as his final resting place: *The man tours both heaven and hell. Each site has elaborate, quite decadent banquets with plenty of food fit for a king and cadres of revelers around the table looking to dig in. Each attendee had silverware that, as it turns out, is connected to their limbs, making it seemingly impossible to feed themselves.*

In hell, everyone only worries about feeding themselves; they are starving.
In heaven, people feed each other and feel joyful and beyond satisfied.

Reflection Questions

*What are the messages you hear about your difference, both
from those close to you and from the outside world?*

How does the media portray those with differences?

Exercise: Movie Audit

When you watch a movie, journal about how characters
with disability (visible and invisible) are portrayed.
What do you notice? What are the words used to describe the
disabled characters? How do other characters react to them?

Compare how those characters with a disability are portrayed versus
those in the movie who are non-disabled and neurotypical.

7

UNINCLUDED

How do we model inclusion when we don't feel included?
Disability needs to be part of the diversity agenda.

In this chapter:

Inclusive leadership is essential. For leaders to be inclusive, they must also feel included and accepted by their teams and organizations. When you don't allow leaders to be their authentic selves, their confidence, effectiveness, and vision can be affected. When disability is left out of diversity conversations, it causes people to hide that part of themselves. To feel that you belong in any given community, it must not only allow you to be yourself but demonstrate its willingness and ability to promote and support your needs.

Feeling Excluded

Scenario 1: The Panel
The panel starts—the topic: Diversity and Inclusion.
I am in the front row, ready to listen and learn.
For thirty minutes, the conversation focuses on race. *Okay. It's important.*
And then, they move to gender, but only as it relates to race. *Okay. This is also important.*
Ten minutes left for the panel. A young Latina woman stands up and shares her story; she is LGBTQ+. *Sexual orientation, another critical aspect of the conversation.*
The session ends.
Where is disability?

Scenario 2: The Speaker
I attend an Inclusion one-day seminar; all of the topics focus on race and gender, except for one Deafblind speaker. She is absolutely incredible, and yet, she is the only speaker who represents any type of disability during the Inclusion Day seminar.
Where is disability?

Scenario 3: The Leader
I am in a meeting about the diversity of leadership in the organization.
Confused, I ask, "Well. What about me? Do you see me as diverse?"
One of them responds, "I guess—you're a woman."
Yes, that is a lens of diversity, I think.
"What about my limb difference?" I ask. "Isn't that part of diversity?"
Several of them say, "Oh, I don't see you 'that way.'"
Frustrated, I think, *This isn't right—I want to be included.*
Where is disability?

Six months after that conversation, one person apologizes.
"I owe you an apology. If you ever said to me, 'I don't see you as black,' I would have had you written up."
I reply, "So why was it okay to say that about disability?"

He shares, "I didn't want to make you uncomfortable or say the wrong thing, but I realize how that might take away from your identity."
I add, "Yes, and it dismisses my experience."

Scenario 4: The Rally
One afternoon, I attend a rally for a couple of hours and enthusiastically listen as speakers express different viewpoints on health justice: young and old, politicians and nonprofit leaders, LGBTQ+, and people of various races and genders. It is powerful.
Something is missing, however. After listening to all those speakers, not once do I hear shout-outs on why health justice matters to those with disabilities.
I contact the organizers and lodge my complaint.
They say, "It was a huge oversight, sorry. Thank you for educating us."
Where is disability?

Insight: Disability is the last frontier
for discussion regarding diversity,
equity, inclusion, and belonging.

Suppose diversity is genuinely about giving a voice to those who have been marginalized. In that case, we need to consider that people with disabilities have a long history of being underrepresented.

When we only focus on specific aspects of diversity—e.g., race and gender—others don't get seen and aren't part of the conversation. Whether intentionally or accidentally, we send the message that their differences don't matter and that they don't belong. In turn, we miss out on their experiences and unique perspective through their lens of intersectionality. If we intend to truly create an inclusive workplace where people feel like they belong, we must be mindful of all aspects of diversity and ensure that *all* voices are heard.

Those with disabilities, the visible and invisible, are the largest minority group. The World Bank estimates that people with disabilities are 15% of the world's population, or one billion people.

Disability belongs in the diversity conversation, yet it's often left out. When we don't include disability, we cannot be genuine when discussing diversity, equity, inclusion, or belonging.

I don't want only to be seen as having a disability. But, I do want it to be acknowledged as a part of me—as well as the fact that I am part of a community that has been marginalized, ignored, and silenced in the past, one that is just as worthy of support and being heard as other similarly mistreated groups. I feel unseen and unheard by not acknowledging my disability in conversations about diversity and other topics that benefit from it, like healthcare.

The actions you can take to be part of the conversation: See me. Acknowledge me. Take time to learn about me and my disability. Ask me questions from a place of curiosity and kindness. Listen as a way to support me.

When you begin paying attention to the absence of disability in these diversity conversations, you start to notice it all the time. It becomes hard to unsee.

Me as a Leader

"Ruth, can we do this?"

"Yes."

I pride myself on never saying no to an idea, though I have shifted some to fit within the mission and vision of what the organization is trying to achieve. I have spent my entire career championing diversity efforts that create opportunities for young people and that will enrich their lives through access to mentoring, education, and career exposure. I've also opened doors for adults to volunteer and share their worlds and expertise with youth. I strive for innovation and creativity to help people succeed. Vision, innovation, and sustainability are the three core principles of how I build organizations.

As someone born with a disability, achievement and solution-focus are my standard operating procedures. I spend my life mastering how to figure things out independently and think outside the box. I am a creative person and consider myself an inclusive leader. I recognize that each person comes in with strengths and areas for growth; I set professional development goals with each person as an individual. As a typical Type A personality myself, I find I work best with people who can take ideas and run with them, people who are action-oriented and self-motivated. The people I want on my team are those who have been challenged, whose life has required them to think outside the box, and who are solution-focused.

I often lead with my head; I am driven and strategic. I spend a lot of time thinking about the external aspects of organizations, building partnerships, raising awareness, and fundraising. I prioritize creating strong working relationships with my staff, board members, and partners. As I reflect on my career, I realize I have inclusion blind spots; I may have missed some of the internal culture aspects, like how to truly include all people so that their voices are heard. I need to slow down to create opportunities for curiosity to take root and for differences of opinion to be resolved, which would help build consensus among various stakeholders. I now understand the importance of representation from different levels of the organization and see the need to create spaces for more inclusive dialogue.

During my career, I rarely share the challenges and experiences of my disability, so my teams don't fully know me. Sometimes, I feel alone and excluded, making it hard to build connections and lead a team.

I think a lot about what makes me an inclusive leader, where I have succeeded, and where I need improvement.

I acknowledge my privilege as a leader and as a white woman.

I understand that not sharing my vulnerabilities affects how others perceive me; sometimes, I may appear silent, removed, and inaccessible.

I see firsthand the juxtaposition between creating a workplace culture where people fit in and how we ask people to show up as their full selves. When we ask employees to fit into a particular culture, we inadvertently encourage hiding.

I have learned that when I share my full self, people feel more connected to me, and then there are safe places for my team members to share their full selves.

Insight: To create a safe place
for sharing, you have to be
vulnerable yourself.

What happens when you are supposed to champion inclusion and don't feel included?

You feel unheard and unseen. You feel defeated.

Leaders need to be seen, too. As a leader, you also want to feel valued and included.

Being an effective leader means caring about the lives and diversity of your employees and team. And it also means employees need to care about the leader and allow them to be human and make mistakes. *When you feel supported, you are able to show empathy and make space for belonging together.*

Belonging is a process. It's about self-acceptance, understanding others, feeling connected and recognizing your voice at the table, and developing empathy for others and their experiences. True belonging requires self-authenticity because that's how we make deep connections. You don't have to hide or fear being rejected or disconnected. It's being part of a group, but it's not groupthink. It's acceptance from others for your similarities and your differences. It allows for working together and connection.

I find that belonging brings out the best in teams and leadership, allowing employees to be seen, and valued for their presence, diversity of mindset, and experience. They can also be more creative and show their full talents and potential when they feel like they belong. Research shows a strong correlation between workplace belonging and increased performance, as well as greater productivity, morale and retention, communication, teamwork, and feeling safe.

Reflection Questions

What topics do you think of when you hear the word diversity?
Who is included? Who needs to be included?

Think about a time you felt included. What were the feelings you experienced?
Think about a time you felt you were being excluded. How did it make you feel?
If you could change that scene, what would you have done differently?
How do you make sure you feel included now?
If you notice others (intentionally or inadvertently) excluding someone, or you feel
someone wants to be part of the conversation but is holding back, what can you do
to try to include that person?

Exercise: Inclusion Inventory

Google an article on diversity from a news outlet.
Create a checklist: Who do they include? Who do they not include?

It comes with a warning: Like most things, you can't unsee it once
you see it.
You will begin to notice more conversations on diversity and who
and what gets included.

PART THREE

UNHIDING

I Get By With A Little Help From My Friends and Family!

Top Left Photo: Dad, Mary, Iris, Carol, me
Top Right Photo: me, Dad, Zippy, Chelsy, Nora
Center Photo (L-R): Cynthia, Dawn, Jenn, me, Renee, Chris, Mary, Nicole
Bottom Left Photo: me, Melissa, Erica
Bottom Right Photo: Kerry, Jenn, me

The Freedom From Unhiding!

Top Left Photo: Zip lining in Belize
Top Right Photo: Catching lunch in Asia
Center Photo: Taking a picture of my hand at LFP weekend with Julie
(photo credit Dean Sanders)
Bottom Left Photo: Trying my hand at the guitar
Bottom Right Photo: Straight shot playing pool

8

CURIOSITY & KINDNESS

**By being curious and kind, we create safe places for people to share.
By being curious and kind, we do away with our assumptions.
By being curious and kind, we allow for connection.**

In this chapter:

One key to unhiding is allowing others to be curious. When paired with kindness, curiosity is one of the most beautiful ways to get to know another person. Curiosity presents itself in many forms—staring, asking, and wondering. One of the most basic ways we gain information is through asking questions. You allow others to choose how and when they share parts of themselves by being curious. When you don't engage with someone with compassionate curiosity, you may assume things about them, leading to misinterpretation and misinformation.

What Happened to Your Hand?

The 'Prityest' Hand

I meet a sweet little seven-year-old girl through my work at a non-profit organization. While she sits patiently in our lobby, waiting for her mom, she says hello and bravely introduces herself as I pass by.

I notice her fidgeting and see that she looks bored. I ask her if she likes to draw, to which she immediately answers yes. I offer her paper and colored pens. She smiles a beautiful, glowing smile. She looks around, figuring out what to draw. She notices my hand.

She quickly asks, "What happened to your hand?"

"I was born this way. We all have something different about us. And, this is what's different about me."

Without missing a beat, she comments, "I like your hand. It's cute."

"That's so nice, thank you." I head back to my office and think to myself that she's just a friendly kid.

Later, as I leave the building to go home, I meet her mom in our lobby. She has bumpy, raised scars on her face and neck, which are pretty noticeable. I imagine this sweet girl has witnessed people staring at her mom.

The little girl hands me a picture with a poem that she made for me.

> *Dear Ruth,*
> *Your hand is the prityest [sic] I have ever seen.*
> *Don't worry.*
> *Look at your hand and say my hand is beautiful.*
> *Say I love my hand.*
> *Please don't worry about your hand, worry only about you.*

I am beyond touched.

I am 28 years old. It's the first time anyone has said that my hand is beautiful. It's the first time anyone has put thoughts about my hand into words.

She is wise beyond her years and understands the beauty of difference far better than others.

On the Playground

I am 48 years old.

At a work picnic in Brooklyn, New York, a seventh-grader runs across the playground to ask me a question. I see him glance at my hand, and I immediately know the look. He blurts out, "Excuse me, miss. What happened to your hand?"

I explain in my usual way, "That's the way I was born. Many of us have different things about us: the shape of our eyes or nose, our bodies."

He nods and gets ready to leave. I notice a slight hesitancy in him, as though he's still thinking; I ask him his age.

"13."

"Wow. When I was 13, I started hiding my hand because I wanted to fit in and look like everyone else; I was ashamed of it."

He nods again, then runs off to join the other kids on the playground.

His mom quickly rushes over and apologizes. "I am so sorry if he asked you anything inappropriate; he noticed your hand and wanted to know what happened. I told him not to ask."

"There is no need to apologize. It's why I love working with kids; they just ask. I am grateful when they ask because it comes from a place of curiosity."

I tell her what I shared with her son.

She's relieved and says, "Thank you. He must have been glad that you took the time to explain it. He is starting to have body image issues; he feels overweight and embarrassed around his peers. He thinks he's fat."

"I understand. Being a teenager can be really challenging because you are so concerned with how you look and so badly want to fit in."

She nods and thanks me again.

I tell her, "Please keep encouraging his curiosity and questions; it's a good thing."

Insight: Children are wonderfully
curious. Encourage and nurture
that mindset in them!

I have shared the message of appreciating childhood curiosity with so many parents who either apologize like that mom or who shush their children and tell them it's not polite to ask.

> When we don't allow for curiosity, we make assumptions and unintentionally perpetuate stereotypes.

Childhood curiosity is a gift and a strength. Kids are exploring and trying to understand difference.

When we silence children from asking questions, we teach them not to be curious. When we silence children around disability, we signal to them that difference is unacceptable and taboo. When we don't allow for curiosity, we make assumptions and unintentionally perpetuate stereotypes.

The Stares

I am in my forties.

I am chaperoning fifteen Black and Brown high school students on a trip to East Asia. As soon as we arrive, it feels like the people in the village's main square, and everywhere we go, stare at us. Initially, we think it's because we are a big group with very talkative teens. And then, stranger things happen. People start taking pictures of the students; they start coming up and touching the kids' skin and hair. The strangers seem obsessed with getting closer. Personal boundaries start blurring. It happens more and more. The students are visibly upset.

The other adult chaperones and I step in and protect the students, saying no to the photos and guarding against the touching. There's not much we can do about the stares.

The students begin to murmur inaudibly at first and then, almost in unison, exclaim, "Ms. Ruth, the people here are racist."

"No, I don't think so." I try to assure them that these people aren't racist.

I naively think, *How could they be racist? The people who live in this country have brown skin.*

"I think it is more that these people see you as different from them, and they are curious. People do and say strange things when they are curious," I add.

The students aren't convinced.

But I know this from my own experience of having one hand.

I decide to open up and share my experience of feeling different—the stares, the whispers, and being touched.

"Do you know how many times a day I feel glaring eyes on my left hand or the quick jerk of the double-takes from people who are embarrassed to be caught staring? Random strangers come up and ask me questions about what happened to my hand, and on more than one occasion, people have reached out and grabbed it. Just wanting to touch it or pray for it."

The students are shocked. Mouths open. They didn't realize. One comes over to hug me. To them, I am just "Ms. Ruth."

I breathe in the relief of my reveal. I expect questions and pushback. Instead, I get embraced with stories.

The students begin to share areas in their lives where they feel different, afraid and alone, and filled with shame.

One girl tells me about her third nipple and her fear of people seeing it and finding it unattractive; a young man tells me he worries because he is so much smaller than his friends that they don't see him as a man; others join in about their body differences that make them feel less than and embarrassed.

We open up the discussion to focus on times when they felt uncomfortable because of being different. A wall between us shatters. Sharing our differences and areas of discomfort cements our connection. It also allows us to mirror positivity, letting one another know our differences aren't awful; they make us unique and beautiful.

Insight: When we start to share parts of ourselves, we discover others' willingness to connect and open up about themselves.

The stares are one of the most challenging and uncomfortable parts of having a visible disability. Someone glances too long at my hand, or looks, is perplexed, then looks away quickly. When this happens, my body reacts; heat rises in my face, and I feel my cheeks turn pink.

It's as though they're judging themselves and me simultaneously. Judging me by asking with an internal voice, "Oh my, what's wrong with her?" Something is not symmetrical. And, questioning themselves, "I shouldn't stare, but I can't look away; something is wrong with the picture—what is it?"

People take huge liberties and break boundaries when noticing people with disabilities, asking questions we don't think to ask others who look different, but somehow, with a disability, it's given the green light:

"Oh my god, what happened to your hand?"
"I am so sorry. Does it hurt?"
"Why don't you get a prosthesis?"

The stares, questions, and touching are rarely predictable; you never know who will do it or when. With this parade of intrusion, it's no wonder that I just wanted to hide, to avoid the discomfort and awkwardness. I learned that life was simpler when I was hiding; no one stared, asked questions, or touched me when I hid my left hand. I felt like I could control and manage the intrusions. But the internal pressure of worrying about being discovered and anticipating the following steps became more time-consuming and more and more exhausting.

We all have differences that we keep hidden. In my work with young people, I have found that my hand has always served as a bridge for understanding, helping them to open up and share their stories. When we share parts of ourselves, we open the space for others to share their vulnerabilities with us.

Thinking Outside the Box

My Gym Trainer

I am 48 years old. It's the first time in my life that I pointedly ask for help for my hand; I ask the front desk staff at my gym for a recommendation for a trainer who can help strengthen my arm. I want someone who won't be afraid of difference and can be creative with their exercises; I don't usually focus on my left hand or arm during my workouts. One of the staff immediately shares a trainer's name who fits that description and customizes workouts in unique ways. I am excited, nervous, and glad I had the courage to ask.

A week later, we meet for our first session.
"What do you want to work on?" she asks.

Sheepishly, I tell her, "I was born missing my left hand, and I hid it for years; I haven't paid attention to strengthening my left arm or defining the muscles."

"Oh, we can definitely do that; let me think a little."

We experiment with a few moves and she tests my movement range and flexibility.

During our next session, she comes armed with a velcro-strap contraption that she invented; it is fitted with a snap hook clip that allows my upper arm to attach to the weight machines. I get to work out and use the weight machines just like everyone else. I begin to strengthen my arm.

By taking my challenge of wanting to lift weights and strengthening my arm seriously, she allows me to feel like I can rely on others to help with my self-development and that I'm able to participate fully. She understands my need and takes the time and interest to create a solution for me. I feel seen and heard.

My Right-Handed Bicycle

When I am six years old, I teach myself to ride a bike without training wheels. My early bike has pedal brakes.

But, as I get older, my adult bike has hand brake clutches on both sides. I can't clutch the left-hand side. I try to ride it anyway, but it feels dangerous not to be able to brake fully with front and back brakes.

So, I take my bike to different shops and nervously ask, "Is there a way to put the brakes on one side?"

"No, no one does it that way," is a constant refrain.

I keep looking for someone who will think creatively, and I find a small bicycle shop with an owner who takes the challenge. He puts all the front and back brakes on my right-hand clutch.

Relief. My challenge is taken seriously. I feel heard.

Insight: Look for creative,
compassionate people who will
help you think outside the box; they
will help to improve your mindset
and sense of belonging.

By being curious and kind and by asking questions to learn more about someone's experience and areas where you can support them, you can help people feel seen and heard, which allows them to feel like they belong and can participate fully in life.

Reflection Questions

Think about a time when you shared part of yourself that you'd kept hidden with someone else.

Are there times when you wanted to share something about yourself and didn't?

When have you been asked a question that made you feel uncomfortable?
What would have made you feel comfortable?
How do you ask other people questions about their differences?

9

FINDING FREEDOM

**Unhiding is being seen.
Unhiding is sharing the most vulnerable parts of ourselves
with others.
Unhiding demands courage and taking risks.
Unhiding is the key to unlocking freedom.**

In this chapter:

Just as developing patterns of hiding does not happen overnight, undoing them—unhiding— takes time. It requires support from others and building a community. There also need to be elements of vulnerability and kindness to oneself—a willingness to challenge the shame one feels and to disagree with internalized harmful or disparaging messages. Unhiding forces us to understand and own our difference, and wrestle with ways to reveal that secret, break down the barriers that keep us feeling disconnected. Often, you need "another hand" to show you how to love and accept yourself—that means letting someone in, finding community, and sharing your story with others. The key to connection and belonging is unhiding.

Telling Men

I don't date much in high school. I like one boy. We have a phone and pen-pal relationship for two years; we talk long distance weekly, and he often sends me lengthy letters. The topic of my hand never comes up. I certainly don't tell him for fear of losing the connection. He never finds out.

As the years move forward, I date men in person. My hand is still in my pocket and rarely gets seen or discussed. I make sure every outfit has pockets, all my dresses and pants; I wear long-sleeved sweaters even in the summer. My obsession with hiding is getting worse, but I get really good at it.

However, there comes the point in dating that I want to let men know. I experiment with ways to reveal my secret.

I am 19 years old. I close the door to my college dorm room and take a few deep breaths. At that moment, I am overwhelmed with feelings of fear, insecurity, and anxiety; I don't know what to expect.

The fear of rejection is real for me.

It is 8:01 p.m., and I let his phone ring three times; I pray that his answering machine picks up. But, no luck. He answers and immediately wants to know what is so important that we have to talk tonight. He is one of the first guys I like in college. He is older; I met him at a party. We date a few times; I hide my hand in my pocket every time and stand to his left in case he wants to hold my hand. I think that I might really like him; this one seems special. He meets my dating criteria: cute, athletic, and a bit of a tough guy but with a sweet side.

"I was born missing my left hand," I blurt out.

I quickly hang up.

I've said it! I feel relief.

I wait and wonder if he will ever call me back.

As the seconds pass, I fear his rejection.

But then my phone rings, and I think, *Oh no, he's calling me back.*

What should I say? I am too scared to answer.

He leaves a message. "Is that all? It so doesn't matter. Call me back!"

It works. I told him, and he doesn't care.

The call, blurt-out reveal, hang up, and wait for the call back becomes my pattern for letting men know, a strategy that spans all potential dates from college through my mid-thirties. It's the test that every potential boyfriend has to take.

It is my test; truthfully, I keep thinking and hoping the next guy will not pass. No one ever fails; they all call back and "don't care" about my hand. Some even try to think about solutions to strengthen it, and some tell me not to hide. But, deep down, I still don't believe I am lovable and I focus on the negative voices in my head rather than the narrative the men tell me.

I continuously question myself and my potential dates.
Who would find me attractive?
Would my physical difference be a deal-breaker?

To me, my hand seems freakish and unbearable to look at. I feel that I will never be asked out again once they find out; I think I will be alone forever.

After college, my friends and I move to New York City, enjoying city life, going out, flirting, and meeting men. Eye contact and youth make it easy. But when it comes to me dating someone, it is always stressful and exhausting.

In addition to the usual, "Does he like me?" and "Will he call me again?", I always have to add, "If he knows about my difference, will he still like me?"

On every single first date, I hide my hand.

On the second and third dates and many after, I hide my hand.

On dates, I always order pasta because it's so much easier to cut with a fork; I don't eat bread because I can't figure out how to butter the bread with one hand; I drink coffee without sweetener because I can only open the packets with my teeth. Even during intimate encounters, the lights are always off, and my hand is always masterfully covered by pillows and sheets.

I hide because I just want the guy to get to know me first without knowing about IT and judging me.

I want to give myself a chance to be liked and found attractive.

I am paralyzed by the fear of rejection and the shame of having such an unattractive part of me.

It is all so stressful.

I convince myself that I will just have to keep flirting and dating rather than try to have a serious long-term relationship.

I deliberately decide to focus my energy on something I can achieve, building a successful career.

I believe in the greatest depths of my psyche that I am unlovable.

Insight: When you build up a lie in your head, you believe it, no matter how damaging or untrue—which can cause you to feel unworthy and unlovable.

I had built such a safeguard, a self-fulfilling prophecy about how others would react to my hand. The walls of distrust don't allow others to reach my heart or change my mind. I never bothered to create a reality check with men. I assumed I was right, that they would not respect my difference and that it was best to hide it from them.

Even years later, there are still moments I struggle with hiding my hand from men. I want to feel safe, and I have equated safety with hiding.

I think about not hiding my hand on dates and sharing it up front on dating profiles. While I imagine I'd probably have fewer men interested, maybe that's okay because they would be the type of men who are accepting, kind, and self-aware, with strong emotional intelligence.

My North Star

I protect myself, put up emotional walls, and have difficulty letting others in. My walls are high—really high.

I am turning 38 years old.

Negative thoughts constantly flood my mind; they try to convince me that no one can love me unless I have two hands. I believe the inner voices that repeat how ugly my little hand is, how it detracts from my beauty.

I think of myself as a misfit.

I hide so that I am seen as normal and beautiful.

It's funny; people say once you stop looking for what you want, you find what you need.

I meet someone who convinces me to get to know my hand, that part of me that's been hidden, neglected, and unloved for so long.

I notice him immediately. He leads a seminar that I sign up for as part of my professional development. He's funny, gregarious, and dynamic.

I laugh at all of his jokes, even the corny ones. He shares his contact information with the entire group when the class ends. I contact him by email under the guise of wanting to continue building out my professional network. We agree to meet up for dinner.

I learn he's someone who understands difference, especially when it comes to hands—he almost lost his hand in a random accident as a teen and had a family member with one hand. He's also curious; he asks questions and listens well. He wants to get to know my hand and me.

Slowly, I allow him in. He follows my lead and lets me get comfortable and set the pace in introducing him to that part of myself I have found so unloveable.

I begin to feel safe.

He touches my little hand. I had never really let anyone touch it. He looks at it and allows me to examine it and take care of it seriously. He embraces it. He normalizes it, and he makes it part of our relationship. He models kindness and teaches me how to cherish my hand and love that part of me that I deemed unlovable. He teaches me how to take care of it, even finding mittens that fit its small size.

After years of neglect and being hidden away, he shows me how to celebrate and love my hand. My hand is sweet and undiscovered. It is the most vulnerable part of myself. It's where I hold the most shame and the origin of so many self-inflicted stories of worthlessness.

He teaches me self-love, how to break down the rigid walls, how to dig through the uncomfortable vulnerability and feelings of shame to own it, embrace it, and release it. He plays a big part in helping me find my whole self. He becomes my North Star on this journey, my Bud. I trust him, and I begin to trust myself as I reconnect with that disconnected part of myself.

Update: After ten years, we end our relationship. It's not because of my hand, but rather because we are at different stages of what we want in life. I take the lessons I have learned and set forth on my own, building my voice and showing love toward myself.

Insight: Sometimes, we need to let
others in to help us learn how to
love ourselves and those parts
that we deem unlovable.

The ultimate love advocate, author and professor Dr. Leo Buscaglia, talks about how you must love yourself first before you can let others love you. I disagree. I think that when you let others in, even one person, to love you, they can teach you how to love those parts of yourself that you find unlovable. That's what happened to me.

Hiding limits our feeling of connection to others and ourselves. I didn't see myself as whole. I didn't recognize my hand as part of me; I didn't let anyone really get to know that part of me, and in turn, I built many walls to protect myself from rejection and hurt. I felt disconnected from people and was not finding love internally or externally. Hiding also caused insecurity. I used sarcasm to keep people at arm's length. Hiding meant there was always a barrier, so people didn't get to know me. It was a form of control. I let people in on my terms—or not at all. It was a test.

When you hide parts of yourself, you're constantly beating yourself up, often wondering, *Why am I still hiding?* You're always thinking, *I shouldn't be hiding; how can I stop?* You don't even notice how many walls you've put up to protect yourself from judgment and rejection. The movie *Maleficent* contains a great example of a person coming to realize that their strategy for self-defense has also

> With every crack in the
> tough walls, I've built
> lightness and joy to fill
> in the gaps.

hurt them. When Angelina Jolie's character finally lets down her walls, when she is loved and lets herself love someone else—only then is she able to accept herself.

The Freedom in Telling the Truth

"You're so brave."

I hear it all the time throughout my life. I am brave because of my hand.

I spent many years feeling like a coward, only sharing what I wanted people to see, not my full self.

Instead, I want people to see me as brave because of my actions toward others, love relationships, advocacy, and travel adventures.

Bravery is about accepting myself and sharing my vulnerability with the world to help someone else. It's venturing out and exploring the world, trying new things, and experiencing different cultures. It's being impeccable with my words and not caving into the fear of being unpopular. It's about being fair. It's bringing up difficult but important conversations and not apologizing when it's not appropriate to do so.

Being brave is being humble enough to learn from my past mistakes and talking about them with others.

I choose to live bravely and decide when to share my experience with others.

When we hide parts of ourselves, we miss out on all that life has to offer: the connections, the experiences, the adventures. We exclude and excuse ourselves from living.

Living authentically to me is being open and honest; following my passion; loving fully; being present in relationships; being imperfect.

We act in ways to fit in, and then we are disappointed when we remain unseen—and are left out. We have to unhide, accept ourselves, and then teach others how to treat us.

Just as living a lie had trapped me, I found momentum in telling the truth.

It can be terrifying to reveal, but it is totally worth it.

I experienced joy again. It's how I got back to living my life.

Sometimes taking a risk and letting someone love that part of your-self that you have deemed unlovable is the greatest gift you can give yourself.

Insight: Unhiding can be scary,
but it's worth it because the world
opens up, and life becomes full
of possibilities.

I know that my difference struck so much shame and fear in me for so many years that I thought I needed to live in hiding, not loving, and I turned more and more inward.

I found that love was a catalyst in helping me accept myself.

With this acceptance came less worrying, less hiding, less insecurity, less loneliness, and less of a desperate need for perfection.

And, I began to accept myself more and have more compassion for others, more connection to myself and the world; I even forgave my parents for the unspoken shame I'd received and the implicit directive to hide.

In full transparency, there are still moments when I get nervous and want to hide my hand, but I know what it's like to be free now, and I can't imagine going back to living with and hiding my secret, back to the shame and fear. I would rather take my chances because finding love is worth it.

Reflection Questions

How do you challenge yourself to own your difference?
How can you make it easier for others to own their differences?
How can you make it easier for others to unhide?

Guided Meditation: A Path to Unhiding

Close your eyes and think about:

What part of yourself do you hide?
What are "the truths" you tell yourself about your hiding?
What would it mean to accept what you're hiding?

What does unhiding look like for you?
Who is helping and supporting you to unhide?

10

REPRESENTATION MATTERS

When we see others who look like us, it can make all the difference. Representation is a critical aspect of inclusion because it allows you to be seen, have your voice heard, and your opinions counted.

In this chapter:

Seeing others who look like you is valuable and powerful. When you don't see yourself represented, you begin to believe that you don't matter. The Disability community needs to continue building representation within various fields and professions so that you can genuinely feel seen, heard, and connected—and know you belong.

A Picnic with Mirrors

I am 48 years old.

Out of the corner of my eye, I notice a woman in the drugstore; she has one arm. I am intrigued. I have started looking for others who have my hand. I really want to talk with her.

I find her in a different aisle.

Awkward at first, I introduce myself. And, instinctively, like a secret handshake, I show her my similar missing hand.

My mind fills with so many questions about her experience. I talk fast and incessantly, blurting out everything. It's like meeting a twin separated at birth; I felt drawn in by someone who looks so similar.

I want to hear about her life and how she handles everything.

I wonder if she has similar thoughts and feelings, a similar kind of shame and fear.

I can't believe I am standing in front of someone else with one hand and talking with her.

This is really the first time since I started accepting my hand as an adult that I am meeting and talking with another person with a missing hand.

She is slightly surprised by my eagerness to connect but asks, "Do you know about the Lucky Fin Project?"

What? Lucky Charms? Wounded Warrior Project?
I have no idea what she is even talking about.

"There's a Facebook group filled with limb-different people just like us."

What's a limb difference? I always refer to it as my little hand.

I run home, leaving behind any purchases I had intended to make, and immediately log on to my computer.

Did she say "Lucky Fin"? Is that the right name?

Whoa!

Suddenly, my screen fills with all these images of kids and people with different types of hands.

Different-shaped and different-sized hands.

Young and old. Kids, parents, adults.

Pictures and stories, triumph and heartbreak.

For the first time in my life, I see my hand on someone else, lots of "someone else's." I have never seen so many limb-different hands; I didn't even know our hands came in all shapes and sizes.

My whole life, I thought I was alone on my own island—so disconnected and so other.

Seeing all these photos with all these hands on display is like looking in a mirror. I learn that The Lucky Fin Project gets its name from the animated character in the movie *Finding Nemo*; Nemo has a smaller, special fin. I haven't ever really paid attention to or felt a connection with the film. This awareness changes that.

It is a paradigm shift, an awakening, realizing that there are other people out there who also have my special hand. There is an online community.

I am not alone.

As I explore more, I notice that the group is holding a weekend event with a picnic outside Detroit, Michigan, in a few months.

I wonder if I should go.

After wrestling with it, I decide yes, of course. I need to explore this path.

July 2017. I nervously rush to the airport amid a torrential downpour; my flight is canceled. No flights are taking off until the next afternoon; by then, the picnic will be over. I am devastated and crushed. As I deal with my sadness, I realize that maybe the universe is letting me know I am not ready for this big step. I think, *Perhaps I'm not really prepared to face my difference.*

July 2018. I try again; this time, all transportation methods cooperate, and I am on my way. Fear and anxiety strike as I am driving from the airport to the weekend event. Even though I am more and more comfortable talking about my hand and embracing how it makes me unique, I begin to worry about how I will react to being with so many people with my hand; how will I differentiate myself now? A flurry of self-doubt enters my mind: What will make me cool? Why am I making myself do this alone? Is it too late to turn around?

When I arrive, the hotel lobby scene is unbelievable—all these people with Lucky Fins.

It's a swarm of hundreds of special hands in all shapes and sizes. It is utterly surreal. I can't stop staring.

There are people of all ages, all races, different genders, and we all have one major thing in common—our unique hands, our limb differences.

Everyone is super friendly and eager to share experiences and struggles with overcoming their challenges. Parents are keen to have their children connect with other kids, feeling relief that their children aren't alone and seeing adults who have grown up with this difference. There is so much positive energy, and this is just the welcome activity in the hotel lobby.

The next day is the picnic. There's a huge field; children are running around. There are organized games. Disney princesses. Barbeques. T-shirts with catchy slogans and beaded bracelets for sale. And lots of people. Over 500 people, all of them here to celebrate limb difference.

As I continue to look around and see all these young kids carefree in their play and the teenagers bonding together, I wonder how my life would have been different if I had had this support and had seen myself like other kids, how much less alone I would have felt. I immediately connect with other adults with limb differences. We start talking and listen to one another's stories; we all have so much more in common than just our physical hands. One of the first things I hear is that some of the adults also hid their hands as kids. It was the first time I realize I hadn't invented hiding; I had spent so many years punishing myself over how bad it was that I hid. I wasn't alone; other people had done it too.

The day is a super-powerful one for me, thanks to the connections I make with others. I feel less isolated, more like part of a community. I am comforted by the shared experiences, realizing I am a role model for the younger people and their parents.

During the evening, we listen to a one-handed guitar player. He blows my mind. I always assumed I could never play the instrument because of my hand, and here was someone making a living at it. He offers me the opportunity to try and play guitar; it's a big step for me, both taking the challenge of playing it and doing so in front of so many people. I feel like a kid trying something new for the first time, but now I am surrounded by supportive people who also never imagined this ability.

As we get ready to leave the next day, one of the fathers of a limb-different child calls my hotel room phone and says how great it was to meet me.

He says, "Ruth, you're not alone anymore."

I start crying hysterically.

It is a wave of relief; I have found my people, my community.
There is no turning back.
I don't have to hide anymore.
I don't have to be alone.
My life is changed forever.

July 2019. I sign up to attend again, and I ask my dad to join me this time.

At first, he seems hesitant to commit and wonders if I really need him to go. That's tough to hear. I have never asked much of my parents, especially regarding my limb difference.

But he thinks it through and agrees to go for me. Though when my flight is severely delayed, he remarks, "Well, maybe I just won't go then."

I feel unsupported, as though he sees it as an obligation, not an opportunity. I can tell he's nervous. He's never really talked to anyone about it or found a community of parents with limb-different children.

But we make it there together. My dad meets other parents and sees the joy and freedom in the kids who attend. He looks like he is enjoying it and appears relaxed. I allow him to take it all in without asking too many questions about his thoughts and feelings during the weekend.

When we finally have a chance to debrief about the weekend, he shares, "It's the first time that I didn't worry about you."

I never knew he worried about me.

"I've always worried about how you would be seen. Would you be loved? Be successful? Would your hand interfere with you having a 'normal life'?"

Wow.

"This was the first time I saw you comfortable with yourself, and I saw others comfortable with you."

Insight: There is power in
community, connection, and finding
those with shared experiences.

Parents worry about their children; I wonder if that concern increases when they have a child with a disability.

I am grateful that I had the opportunity to share that experience with my dad and thankful for the community I have found.

It's an interesting feeling to be around people when you don't have to explain your difference. By seeing people similar to you, you feel less alone and are better able to appreciate your difference; you learn to accept it as a part of you.

I only wish my mom had known there was a community she could've been part of, too; she might have accepted that my little hand wasn't her fault. With all of my mom's external perfection, I often felt I was a reminder of imperfection. She didn't know how the world would accept me, as she only had external messages about beauty. And, disability wasn't seen as beautiful.

After my parents' divorce and before she got sick with dementia, my mom and I enjoyed some healing time together. I shared with her that I never blamed her for my hand; I just wanted a place to talk about it. Though we never talked about "the book" she tried to give me, I understood how she struggled for ways to bring up the topic and how alone she felt. She just wanted me to feel normal. Unfortunately, she passed away, still blaming herself for taking the sedative when she was pregnant with me, never knowing there were so many other moms just like her and that she didn't have to be so alone.

It was only after my mom's death in October 2015 that I felt I could deeply explore my issues around my hand for the first time without the guilt of hurting her. Now, I feel free to share and open up about my difference and call it a disability. Through this process, I start to understand her better and learn to accept myself.

I forgive her.

Because, to me, forgiveness is about letting go. It's part of the grief cycle. It's part of self-acceptance. Forgiveness is about understanding and empathy—it's a way of opening your heart and finding freedom to unleash the things holding you back.

Same Same, But Different

I have been afraid to identify as someone with a disability for much of my life. I never actually called it a disability.

I worked so hard to fit in with the able-bodied world that I denied my disability and put up blinders in recognizing those with differences.

I only remember seeing a few people with a disability like mine:

> My horseback riding teacher at camp had only one hand.

> The doctor with one hand who wore a hook prosthesis.

> A guy playing pool with one hand. A friend suggested we go talk to him.

I remember wondering why they were showing their hands.

I couldn't relate because I wasn't comfortable with that part of myself, and I hadn't found my path to acceptance.

As I build my comfort by showing my hand, I start to accept my hand, and my desire to connect with others who look like me grows.

I begin to notice and connect with everyone who has a limb difference. I spot them everywhere, even the ones who are still hiding.

The guy who stops me on a train because he saw my unhidden hand. He reveals his hand underneath a sweater; he's in his forties and still hiding. He asks me how I stopped hiding.

The guy I meet poolside in Puerto Rico who, even on his wedding day, kept his hand hidden; his soon-to-be bride has never seen it. He asks me how I stopped hiding.

The woman in the military who enlisted despite her limb difference; she's not hiding, but asks me when I stopped hiding.

The list goes on.

It's as though the universe starts to place people in my life to showcase all the different reactions and coping mechanisms of people with limb differences.

After seeing all the faces on the Lucky Fin Project website, I grow even more curious and wonder, *Does this online world exist in other ways?* I find a website called *The Mighty*, dedicated to people sharing about disability; I search through it and read about people with limb differences, their humanizing stories, and how they share so many of the same feelings of hiding and shame. I can't believe others have had similar feelings.

I read on the website about those who hid their hands, those who didn't, and those who used activities like sports and theater to keep themselves from hiding.

And most share about their need to overachieve through academics, athletics, and in their career.

Many people comment about hating the stares and the bullies.

My only bully when I was a kid was a girl in first grade. My dad went to the school and dealt with it immediately.

I have a strange reaction to all my reading and newfound community.

I begin to question if my own story is any different.

Was I even so special?

But the more I explore, the more connections I find, the more fascinated I am to hear how we all experience our life with limb differences. And even though we have similar differences, we have experienced them in unique ways.

The connections light up my world.

It's as though the universe keeps shining light on my path.

The more I meet others with disabilities, the more connected I feel and the more joy I experience. I feel less alone.

I begin to feel like, in taking this journey, learning about others' lives, I am collecting puzzle pieces that will eventually reveal to me the whole picture, my life's purpose. The more I am on the right path, the more puzzle pieces I receive.

Insight: Only when we are being genuinely vulnerable can we find true connection. Connections to others allow us to feel less alone and find community.

There are so many interesting people out there. When you allow yourself to be open, connections to other people happen more and more. People want to share their stories with you.

The Power of Seeing Someone Who Looks Like You

I am 48 years old.

Watching the National Football League (NFL) Draft is not typically how I spend the weekend, but Saturday, April 28, 2018, was unique.

For me, the event is one of hope, nervousness, and legitimacy—all bundled together.

The anticipation of a young football player waiting to get picked for a team reminds me on a much smaller scale of my childhood hope and anxiety of waiting to get selected for kickball teams year after year in elementary school.

The NFL Draft, like elementary school, is a showcase of athleticism, popularity, and statistics, with the more athletic kids always getting chosen first.

I almost didn't want to watch.

The big question for me: Would Shaquem get drafted?

Shaquem Griffin, the one-handed football player from Florida, dreamed of playing professional football from a young age. Shaquem Griffin was often sitting on the sidelines because people told him that football players need two hands. Shaquem Griffin never gave up and worked to prove that he is able.

Would someone give Shaquem a chance, not because of his missing hand, but because of his ability, determination, and strength?

During the fifth round, he is drafted.

Salty tears run down my face. A sigh of relief. A massive glimmer of hope.

Shaquem's draft pick is critically important to me.

Insight: Just seeing one other
person who looks like you can
make all the difference.

Like the story that went viral in 2018 of the little girl who was in awe of seeing Michelle Obama's portrait painting at the National Portrait Gallery, I am in awe of Shaquem being drafted into the NFL.

I applaud Shaquem for never giving up; I imagine what courage it must have taken him to persist, and I understand his drive. I applaud Nike, Toyota (for their Paralympics commercial), and the NFL for beginning the conversation on difference and ability by having an active, public voice and taking action.

As someone born with a limb difference myself, I understand part of Shaquem's experience in a unique way. Though he and I are different people and come from different backgrounds, we share a piece of common knowledge and language—people think we "can't" because of our limb difference.

We learn to live with discomfort.

Strangers stare at our missing hand and ask questions like, "Oh my God, what happened to your hand?"

People make assumptions about our abilities all the time.

We are often in a position to prove that we can do things, and we have to overachieve because we don't want to be overlooked or defeated.

We have had to figure out how to live in a two-handed world with ease and lack of dependency.

Seeing someone who looks like me and owns it proudly inspires me. Shaquem's draft pick helps me change the way I view myself.

Seeing someone for the first time in my adult life receive national attention, sign a Nike deal, and get picked by a top sports franchise, gives me hope.

Hope for me. I have felt unseen for so long.

Hope for the current and future generations of kids born missing a limb so that they experience feeling valued.

Hope that we can start an honest conversation about difference and abilities, both in this country and worldwide.

I have been learning that our differences make us unique and are our greatest gift to share—they make us stronger.

Looking for Representation

The VHS Tape

I am 21 years old.

My dad's boss shares with us a VHS tape recording of an interview with a Los Angeles TV newscaster with webbed hands named Bree Walker. It was the first and only time I saw someone on TV who looked different physically.

I am amazed.

I admiringly watch her, noticing her very public display of her hands; she has a very front-facing career. And in the interview, they mention that she is married to a very handsome sportscaster.

I am hopeful, thinking perhaps my difference will not exclude me from career, love, and acceptance.

The View

I am 30 years old.

Debbie Matenopoulos leaves the TV show *The View*.

I find the courage to write to Barbara Walters—and advocate to fill the vacant host spot with someone with a physical difference. It doesn't happen.

I am disappointed. All I want is to see someone who looks like me on national television as a role model. For disability to be seen as normal.

Childish Gambino

I am 49 years old.

The Internet is abuzz with the video *This Is America* by the rapper Childish Gambino; it poignantly represents serious recent tragedies and resilience in the face of oppression and violence—it is deep and heavy, courageous, and filled with subtle and not-so-subtle messages. The video is powerful because it calls attention to how Black lives are often devalued and left out of the conversation in America.

I wonder who is standing up, expressing outrage, and representing those with disabilities as courageously and controversially.

Insight: We need strong advocacy
to see difference represented.
Representation matters.

When we don't see anyone who looks similar to us physically, we carry shame and fear about our difference. However, the truth is that our differences are what make us interesting and unique; they are our gift and our life purpose, yet so often, we try to hide them to make ourselves fit into a fictionalized stereotype of what "normal" is. Difference is the norm.

People with physical differences have been marginalized for generations. Often, our difference makes people uncomfortable, and we are required to cover up. People with disabilities rarely appear in starring roles on television, in movies, or even in music, yet we are a significant part of the general population. We don't have anyone starting hashtags for award shows like #soablebodied.

I am left wondering: How can we find our media champions and advocates to initiate campaigns around difference—*all* difference? Who in Hollywood and the media will take a real chance to include those with disabilities? How do we build a community around differences? Real advocacy demands risk and courage. Accepting our differences and those of the people around us takes boldness and heart.

I acknowledge there are some exceptions, most notably how the deaf community has recently had some important representation in Hollywood, as movies like the Sound of Metal and CODA won significant awards in 2021 and 2022. I look forward to seeing continued advocacy and action towards the positive portrayal of those with disabilities both in front of and behind the camera.

Reflection Questions

When was the first time you saw yourself represented? How did you feel?
When do you feel genuinely connected to others?

What does community mean to you?
Where have you found your community?

11

BUILDING EMPATHY

Empathy requires curiosity.
Empathy requires listening.
Empathy builds connection.

In this chapter:

You discover that empathy is about being able to hear how someone else is being challenged and listening to what they need. Empathy requires curiosity and the desire to understand others' experiences.

Finding Someone Who Listens

Given that, for much of my life, I never talked about my hand, I seek out places where I can talk about my feelings and thoughts. I had been to therapy previously, but now I look for a therapist with the express purpose of digging into and uncovering the reasons I hid my hand. I want to understand how I built those negative messages and what kept me hiding all those years.

Finding a good therapist is hard work. You want someone you can build trust with, someone who is curious and listens to you.

I am in my late forties. I find and fire four therapists in a row.

First therapist. Older white male; his first-floor office is in a beautiful, classic prewar building on the Upper East Side in New York City. It's decorated with old-fashioned, formal-style wingback chairs. He sits far from me, creating our first barrier. He begins the session with the typical question, "So, what brings you here?" I go into detail, telling him about my hand and that I am looking to understand why I hid it. After my long narrative, he responds, "That's a great story, but we will not talk about your hand in here. It's called reaction formation. You hid your hand for so long and didn't talk about it; now, the natural tendency is to focus on it. That's not healthy." I fire him.

Second. Middle-aged white female; her messy, cluttered office is in midtown Manhattan, filled with disorganized books and random mismatched furniture. She asks the same question, "Why are you here?" Unlike the first therapist, she engages in the hand discussion right away and shares a connection to someone she knows who also has one hand. She even encourages me to write a book about my hand. But something is off. She keeps chewing on her hand, clipping the cuticles with her teeth. It is distracting. I am here to talk about my hand, and all she and I could do is focus on hers. Fired.

Third. A 90-year-old female therapist who only wants to talk about my hand and the sexual intimacy I have with men. Not that that is not interesting, but that's not why I am here. Fired.

Fourth. Middle-aged female therapist whom I had previously seen years earlier when my mom first got diagnosed with dementia. She is into alternative therapy, meditation, and hypnosis. I hadn't been ready for her earlier, but now I think I have evolved as I have developed my journaling and meditation practice. Things are going relatively smoothly, and several sessions in, we are talking about whether I should show my hand or not during dating. She suggests role-playing on how I can bring it up and how to handle it if someone has an adverse reaction to me telling them about my hand. She plays me, and she gets more and more frustrated by these imagined men and says I need to get mad and tell them off. I tell her that's not my style. Again, she repeats, you need to get angry. I feel that she isn't hearing me and allows her own emotions to get in the way. It's also not why I am here. Fired.

Insight: Be okay with asking for
what you need and continuing
to pursue it. Trust your gut.
Don't settle.

I end up going back to my therapist, whom I'd seen for years. I searched for other therapists because I didn't think he would explore past trauma; he always seems to stay more present in our sessions together. I was wrong. He allows me to create space for questions and teaches me how to do that with men. He understands why I hid and also helps me with the tools for revealing. He also wonders if I have had conversations about my hand with my dad, my first male role model.

He asks, "What does your dad think about your hand?"

I tell him I have no idea. He feels that it's a critical piece of the puzzle in my search to understand why I hide my hand from men.

I call my father and ask him about my hand—what were his thoughts and feelings when I was growing up?

We acknowledge we have never talked about it. He's open to talking. He fills in much information that I have forgotten or never knew, like my birth, the first-grade bully, and the concerns he and my mom had. He shares so much rich information about me and how they treated me as normal. We bond over the conversation and start to talk about my hand more often. He begins to understand how it would have been helpful for me to talk about it during my childhood and lifetime.

I learn that, sometimes, the support you needed was where you started, but you need to explore to find out the grass isn't always greener.

Step into My Shoes

After watching Chimamanda Ngozi Adichie's TED Talk: The Danger of a Single Story and understanding how she finds her voice and how we need to listen to people's experiences to get to know them, I wonder what I wish people knew about me.

I want people to know how much I fight to be perfect, out of a fear that people will think less of me because of my disability. Sometimes I wonder what it would be like if my family, friends, and colleagues would bandage their left hand in a ball for one day to lose its functionality; could they begin to understand my world?

I continue to wonder.

How would they handle the stares of random people at the grocery store while they tried to balance the shopping basket?

Would they understand my drive to be a Type A personality as a need to control my environment and be seen as ultra-capable?

Would they appreciate my desire sometimes to tuck my hand away and hide it so that nobody would look, nobody would stare, nobody would ask, and nobody would judge?

In that short time frame, would they realize how many solutions I have had to come up with to compensate for living in a two-handed world?

Would they understand my newfound desire to share my difference out loud?

Moreover, would one day in my shoes be enough to understand all my experiences and what makes me me?

And, what if I thought more universally instead of focusing on myself?

Could I try and put myself in someone else's shoes for the day?

How would I understand their experience?

How would I handle the complexities of that person's life, and would it provide me with a different way of thinking about other people in the world?

Insight: Sometimes, we need to step back and truly try to imagine ourselves in another person's situation to better understand their struggles and desires, as well as our own.

My literal shoe size is 8.5, but my figurative shoe size is much more significant. Walking in my shoes includes the baggage I carried for years as someone who hid my limb difference from the world—the fear, the obsession, the paranoia, and the shame. My secret was my disability. And today, my shoes are also filled with the reality of still having a missing hand, learning to accept it, and building the courage to flaunt it.

Can we ever really put ourselves in someone else's shoes, to understand another's bias and our own?

With all the DEIB training on bias, I've wondered if an afternoon is enough to change a mindset, initiate a more extensive national discussion on difference, and cover all the facets of diversity? I imagine not, but perhaps it's a beginning.

What if I were (fill in the blank) for the day: What would I understand differently? How would it shape my worldview? What would I want people to know, think, and advocate for me?

The questions can differ based on each person's experience. The answers form the lens through which we understand one another and our world will vary as well, and they may restrict us from understanding others' experiences fully because of our bias.

Empathy, Not Judgment

I am 52 years old.

For several weeks in a row, I avoid bringing up a difficult subject with a friend and let several calls go unanswered.

"I feel like you're being distant. Is something wrong?" my friend asks tentatively as we begin our phone conversation.

I pause and wonder, *Do I tell her the truth, or continue to hold back?*

I am not prepared for this. I have nothing rehearsed.

I take a deep breath and decide to share my thoughts—she's one of my best friends.

"I don't understand the decisions you are making about your mom's care; I am really disappointed in your choices," I blurt out.

She's shocked. She starts to share her reaction to my feedback.

I'm not really listening. I am clouded by my own version of her story and the assumptions I have already made; everything she says sounds like just an excuse. I think that I know better because of my own experience of taking care of my mom and ultimately losing her.

We are at an impasse. I shut down emotionally, and so does she. We hang up the phone and are both left with feelings of frustration and sadness. We take some space.

After the call, I journal about my feelings and thoughts. Through my introspection, I realize how differently I could have handled the situation. I recognize how I could have slowed down my internal thoughts to let her talk, been curious and asked questions to understand her actions, and shown empathy because this was her experience, not mine.

A few weeks later, we talk again. She shares her hurt and her thoughts. I apologize for not letting her tell her story and for being judgmental. She appreciates how I now listen and hear her.

Insight: To truly show empathy toward others, we need to put aside (momentarily) our own stories and experiences that can cloud our ability to listen and be present.

Just as I want others to understand and not judge my experiences, I realize the work I still need to do to create empathy and connection with others.

Some of the keys to building genuine empathy include a desire to understand the other person and ask about their experience; when we add listening to that equation, we build genuine empathy.

Empathy isn't as simple as putting yourself in someone else's shoes because we can't ever truly do that. It's not about just saying that you understand and want to be there for someone.

Empathy is about hearing how someone else is being challenged and listening to what they need. Empathy requires curiosity, compassion, and being open-minded, so you can ask, listen, and understand someone's experience.

Empathy creates opportunities for people to be seen and feel connected.

Empathy allows us to learn and grow from one another.

Reflection Questions

Where do you seek support and ask for what you need?
When do you feel comfortable walking away when your needs aren't being met?

How do you show empathy? How do you want others to show you empathy?
Think about a time when you did not show empathy; how could you next time?

Exercise: In Your Shoes

Instead of always discussing diversity through an intellectualized lens, what if you try to experience other people's differences firsthand? Here's a preliminary list.

(Note: I recognize the implicit privilege that we have in being able just to wonder.)

What if:

1. What if you were a different race: Would you understand racism differently? Would you comprehend the effect of stereotypes and stigmas differently? Would you gain a deeper understanding of privilege?

2. What if you were a different gender: Would you be able to understand the importance of breaking the glass ceiling and of the #metoo movement? Would you question your past behavior? Would you be worried about the future rights of your gender?

3. What if you were LGBTQIA+: How would you understand sexuality differently? Would you understand the need for marriage equality through a different lens? Would you understand the dissonance that comes from dealing with gender dysphoria and the difficulty of coping with that sense of alienation from your physical self? Would you be more sensitive to those in various stages of self-discovery and understanding and be able to support them better?

4. What if you had a physical difference that you couldn't hide: Would you understand beauty differently? Would you come away with an understanding of how superficial and difficult dating can be?

5. What if you were severely overweight: Would you stop judging people's ability based on looks? Would you realize the

discomfort of people's stares? Would you want to redefine society's standards of beauty?

6. What if you had depression: Would you understand the struggle to even get out of bed some days? Would you understand the desire to end your life? Would you come to recognize its different forms, that being "high functioning" isn't a good indicator of one's mental well-being?

7. What if you had other mental health issues: Would you stop stigmatizing those whose brain chemistry is not in their control? Would you understand the power of the mind differently?

8. What if you had an addiction: Would you better understand temptation and gratification? Would you understand the power of "the high"? Would you realize that it's a disease? Would you better understand and empathize with the senses of shame, denial, and desperation that can arise from addiction?

9. What if you had a difficult childhood: Would you better understand the unseen scars that can be left over, and the effects on relationships? Would you understand anger and sadness differently? Would you be better equipped to recognize others' "strange" reactions to certain situations or stimuli to be rooted in childhood trauma?

10. What if you were a foster child: Would you understand the difficulties of the child welfare system and how a child can be a perpetual victim in the hands of adults? Would you understand disappointment differently? How would your understanding of trust, family, and authority be different?

11. What if you were a veteran: How would you understand post-traumatic stress disorder? Would you understand the power of war and death more intimately? Would you experience fear and bravery in the same instant? Would you have mental and physical wounds, some of which you could and couldn't explain to civilians or not want to talk about at all?

CONCLUSION: GIVE ME A HAND

Sometimes, you just need a helping hand.
To build understanding.
To build connection.
To build representation.
To build empathy.
To own your difference.

In this chapter:

Becoming your whole, authentic self is something that cannot be done alone—it takes community and connection to others. It requires working on yourself, being vulnerable and trusting, and letting others in. Only when you own your difference can you truly be there for others. The irony: you can't do this *singlehandedly*.

The Circle of Truth

I am 52 years old.

I walk toward the Red Circle.
People are here to listen to my "idea worth spreading."
My talk is: *When I Stopped Hiding, I Found Freedom.*
I take a deep breath and own that I am at TEDx.
I tell my story.
I share my difference, my disability.
I feel relief for fully unhiding on this platform.

Day after day, I wait for it to go live online. Any day now.

It's live. Oh my!
Nervously I watch it, and I begin to cry.
My story is out there.
It's beautiful. I can't stop crying. It's my story, and it's gorgeous.
I share it with friends, family, and my network.
I watch the video views start growing.
I start to receive messages from around the world.
A woman tells me this is her story, too; she thought she was alone for 50 years.
A mom can't wait to show it to her daughter, who's been starting to hide in high school.
A dad shares his own daughter's difference and disability.
Messages come pouring in about hiding, feeling alone, and gratitude.

I feel I am really seen for the first time.
I feel like I have something to offer the world. I belong.

Insight: Being truly seen and
accepted is the goal. It's
about Belonging.

Why is it important to be seen?

When we don't feel seen:
We don't feel heard.
We don't feel valued.
We don't feel connected.

When we feel seen:
We share our voices and are heard.
We are open about our differences and are accepted for our strengths and our challenges.
We get to unhide.

TEDx: When I Stopped Hiding, I Found Freedom
https://www.ted.com/talks/
ruth_rathblott_when_i_stopped_hiding_i_found_freedom

Singlehanded No More

Sometimes, you just need a hand, literally and metaphorically.

As you learned through reading my stories, I spent many years trying to unhide on my own. I tried to take my hand out of my pocket and unhide on numerous occasions. When I would start new situations, I pleaded with myself to make this time different: *Don't hide.* It never worked. I faced the same obstacles repeatedly. Even when I came up with other solutions, my mind always convinced me to go back to hiding. I had created a distorted sense of reality and couldn't trust my own mind for self-evaluation and self-acceptance. The messages were so ingrained.

I built a fortress of protection and distrusted others with my secret, my shame; I couldn't imagine a world where I felt accepted and secure. I felt alone, destined to keep hiding that part of myself; this was my way of life. I didn't think I needed help, or even understand how much help I needed; I had been doing things for myself for so long that asking for support seemed unnecessary. It's hard to suddenly ask for help when you've had to rely only on yourself for so long.

Many of us create a false narrative, whether it's for a physical difference like mine or about differences in gender, ethnicity, sexual orientation, age, religion, family background, or education. We cling to it, making it hard to stop hiding because we believe it to be absolute truth and fear judgment from others.

> Our differences are the keys to unlocking our purpose; they are our gift.

For years, I taught myself to disconnect that "different" part of me; I did not own it. I made my life so hard, always having to prove how capable I was, both physically, through carrying everything myself and overachieving, and emotionally, by not letting people know how tough things were for me. Proving oneself takes a lot of energy; you are overcompensating all the time—always anticipating and forecasting how you will handle your next challenge. You never get to relax. You never get just to be you. You're always worried about when someone will find out what you're hiding and wondering what they'll think. It was exhausting and lonely.

But, little by little, when I let someone else in and let them guide me, it took some of the pressure off me. I connected with myself and slowly let others in, too. I realized that my hand *was* part of me, but it wasn't *all* of me. I had to understand it from a very elementary level, like my blue eyes are part of me, my belly and my breasts are part of me, but they aren't all of me. By understanding how to love my hand, it became part of me; it became connected to me—my full self. I learned how to love my hand. I began to accept myself.

And then, I started to connect with others who looked like me, and I became curious; I listened in on conversations between people wrestling with similar things and realized I wasn't alone in my thinking. I wasn't the only person hiding parts of myself. I wasn't the only one struggling.

I found I wasn't connecting with people because I was not connecting with myself. I was so busy hiding, forecasting my next steps, and overachieving that I never got to just be present in a relationship with myself or others. Connecting with others is super important because it helps end the distortion in your mind. You begin to change those voices, those inner demons that tell you how ugly something is about yourself or how much shame you hold; you break those voices by countering them with positive words about yourself.

Once I began to connect with others, I started to talk about my hand and share parts of my experience; it made me vulnerable. As I got comfortable with myself, people felt comfortable with me. They started sharing their stories of difference and hiding and shame and challenge; the more sharing I did and the more vulnerable and authentic I was, the more it made people connect with me. There is real power in sharing your difference.

> Learn about my difference and work to understand it. Share your difference with me. This is how we build community.

Things start getting easier when you finally find the courage to let your guard down and ask for help. I learned it was okay to ask for help and that not everything had to be a challenge; I didn't have to have a superpower to prove I was capable. Sometimes, just letting someone else do something for you is a gift.

To ultimately destroy the compulsion to hide and find a way to accept ourselves fully, we require connection. It's about letting others in, listening to the positive messages others give you about your difference, and letting someone show you how to love yourself because we often don't know how to do that for ourselves. It's like we each need to give a hand to one another so we can all rise to the next level.

Insight: We can't unhide alone.
The key to unhiding is connection, and
the key to connection is unhiding.

You never get to be your authentic self when you hide because you're always worried about someone discovering your secret. We hold so much shame around our difference. We have had to prove that we can overachieve to break the stereotype and the self-stigma we have created about our difference.

That's the gift of unhiding: you get to be yourself, you get to ask for help, and you get to be present. And, by being present, you form authentic connections and think about the future differently. When you unhide, your mind is free from many of the challenges and issues that kept you living in fear; you're able to be present and experience your five senses. There's a grounding in unhiding because you're not worried about everything or everyone else.

Unhiding makes me a better friend and a better leader because I can be truly present and connected to others, and I recognize I don't have to handle everything on my own.

We all need support, and that can show up in various ways. For me, it meant meeting someone who taught me how to love that part of myself I deemed unlovable for so long, connecting with others who looked like me, and sharing my journey. It's also about therapy, doing the work on yourself because you want your situation to be different, and being willing to make the changes. I got my life back, but I couldn't have done it by myself.

We all have the power to unhide and own our differences, and we don't have to do it alone. It takes support from others.

When people say to me, "Oh, Ruth, you're so amazing. You overcame this challenge," I let them know that I didn't do it alone. I had a group of people around me who loved and supported me, who I allowed in even when I didn't feel so lovable. They helped me own my difference. I felt connected.

For that, I'm grateful.

I thank my parents for pushing me forward. Yes, I wish we had talked about it. I wish they had modeled what talking about challenges looks like and asked questions about my feelings. These are things I learned so that I could help others.

In my work with young people and families, I encourage conversation, particularly with kids with disabilities. Disability is not frightening. I think parents fear labeling a child, but the truth is that a child with a disability, at some point, will figure out they are "different," and they will need a space to talk about how it affects them.

There is real power in sharing your difference and your feelings about being different.

> When we share our vulnerability, other people have space to share their stories and vulnerability.

As I got comfortable with myself, people got comfortable with me, and they started sharing their stories of difference, hiding, shame, and challenge.

I share my story so that others can start sharing theirs.

Own Your Difference

I'm in the early stages of working with an executive leadership coach; I struggle to understand my life purpose and how to weave my desire to incorporate my limb difference into some aspect of my work. When we meet, I toggle between wanting to talk about it and just being satisfied that I'm not hiding it much anymore. I am unsure how much I want to own it publicly. I lack clarity and question whether I should even pursue talking about my disability. I know it's important, but I question whether I have the commitment to follow my passion. I think we are both frustrated at the impasse and unsure of the next steps.

"You keep talking about your hand; who even cares about it?" she asks pointedly and without emotion.

> What? How dare she! I am furious and hurt.
> My eyes swell with tears.
> I can't believe she would ask me, "Who cares about your hand?"
> I take a few weeks off from our work together.
> I don't answer her calls.
> I want to stop working together.
> I so badly want to tell her off.

But, as I cool down and reflect, I talk to friends and journal about her question: *Who cares about your hand?* I realize that she isn't asking to be hurtful; instead, she asks because she wants me to own it and take a stand. She needs my purpose to be important to me before I can make it important to anyone else.

Insight: We need to own our
differences before we can
ask others to do so.

I needed to be confident that my difference matters to me because there would be people along the way who would not care, who would challenge me as to why this was important; I needed to care about my difference more than anyone else.

If I didn't fully lean into embracing my hand and my journey, no one else would. I had to convince myself it was necessary before expecting that from others. I would have to defend it. I might be alone, but I would have myself and my strength. When we ask others to see us a certain way, we need to see ourselves that way first—we can't be half in with owning our difference when we are doing advocacy work.

It's all about owning your difference. That's universal.

I have learned that the most powerful gift you can give yourself is owning your difference—which is the key to unlocking shame. It's the end of hiding. It's unhiding.

When we own our differences and share them with others, we connect with people.

They start to tune into their own areas of difference and share their stories.

I've experienced it **firsthand**.

When we own our differences, it's easier to quiet the negative voices in our heads.

Even when others say cruel things, owning our difference reminds us of our worth.

When we own our differences, we give them strength and ability; we give them power.
We get to choose when and how our differences show up and when we want to share them on our own terms with the world.

When we own our differences, we connect with others.
We share our vulnerability so other people can see and share theirs.
We build community by owning our gifts, our uniqueness.
We increase community, inclusion, and belonging.
That's how we come together.

> Be true to yourself;
> get to know yourself
> and love yourself first
> so that you know who
> your true self is.

Imagine if we all started to share our differences and fully own them. Imagine that world!

Me, Now

This woman is me.

I was born with a limb difference.

Growing up, I was shy and sweet. I was carefree.

At 13, I developed a secret that would stay with me for 25 years. I found myself enveloped in shame.

I was a magician and a con artist, fooling those around me into thinking I had two hands instead of one. Hiding became my obsession.

I was afraid if people found out about my hand, I would never keep love, not make friends, not get hired–afraid people would find me ugly.

Until one day, I met someone who taught me how to cherish my difference, how to take care of it and look at it, and how to love those parts of me I found unlovable. I learned how to love myself.

I then found a group, a community of others who shared my limb difference. I unhid more.

Even though I stopped hiding my hand physically, I found that I was still hiding because I wasn't sharing my story—when nobody knew where I was coming from, I felt excluded.

So, I started sharing my story and found that, when I did, others began sharing their stories of difference with me in response.

Now, I use my strong voice to expand diversity to include those with visible and invisible differences.

I am grateful for my difference; it makes me unique and beautiful, and it's my gift—a way to connect with others. My superpower is building relationships with others.

I boldly keep an open heart and gain courage from self-acceptance.

I see myself as whole and understand that true beauty is found in authenticity.
And there are moments I still think about wanting to hide. It's a continuum.

When I unhide, I experience joy again; I get back to living my life.

I have been an award-winning CEO of a nonprofit organization.
I have traveled around the world and taken thousands of selfies with my hand.
I have been in love and had my heart broken.
I have amazing friends and family who cheer me on.
I have courage—to dream, to be creative, and to be different.

Unhiding allows me to be fearless, form authentic connections with others, and take risks with confidence.

Unhiding allows me to be who I truly am. It allows the outside world to redefine diversity in ways that include people like me!

When I stopped hiding, I found freedom.

And, the best is still to come!

Reflection Questions

Do you feel you're ready to unhide or help someone else unhide?
If not, what would help get you ready?
If so, what's going to be your first step? Where will you seek support?

If we were to reach full inclusion and belonging in society:
What would your life look like?
What would your workplace feel like?
What would leadership look like?
How would you start to value others' differences?

For Leaders and Managers Interested in DEIB:

The C.U.R.E. to Inclusion is a model I built for workplace inclusion focused on four key dimensions: *Connection, Understanding, Representation, and Empathy,* which all lead to *Belonging.*

1. We begin by understanding our own differences; we get comfortable with the areas where we have held shame and hidden parts of ourselves. We share and model vulnerable conversations for others.

2. We initiate our discovery process about other areas of difference. We proactively do our learning and begin listening to others and their experiences. We drive connection.

3. We examine our circles and teams and think about representation; whose voices we are hearing and whose we are not.

4. We build empathy and trust by listening, validating, and letting others know we hear and see them. We listen so that people feel included and accepted.

Belonging is at the heart of the process. When we create space for safe conversations and build inclusive workplace environments, employees increase productivity, are more team-oriented, and have greater loyalty to the organization—they feel that they belong, and so will you.

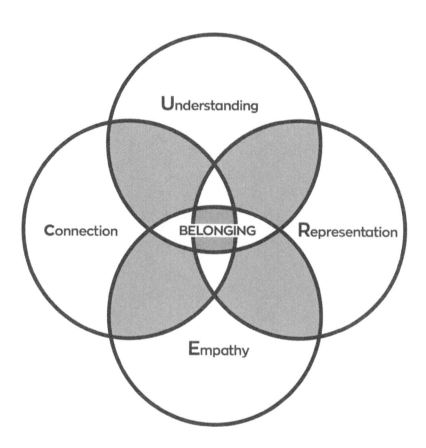

Copyright Ruth Rathblott, 2022

NEXT STEPS

Thank you for following me on my journey. I didn't want to leave you here without the next steps for you.

Just as unhiding my hand took me many years and outreach of support from different areas of my life, I recognize that you may also be on a journey and be looking for a roadmap.

If you are **someone who has a disability,** whether visible or invisible, I want to help you think through your journey to unhiding and finding support systems. I have created a series of reflection questions to consider as you take the next steps forward.

If you are a **parent/guardian of a child** with a disability, you have the unique opportunity to help you and your child navigate the path of disability support together. A resource tool on my website can help initiate those conversations.

If you are a **workplace leader** looking to expand the diversity conversation and build an inclusive work environment, I have outlined a roadmap for creating those critical next steps for DEIB.

All these tools are available as a downloadable pdf on my site: ruthrathblott.com.

GRATITUDE

**"If you want to go fast, go alone.
If you want to go far, go together."**

—African proverb

My incredible friends and family for being on this journey with me and allowing me to embrace connection. You encourage me to own my difference and share my story. I couldn't have unhid without you.

The Lucky Fin Project for helping me find my community.

My Bud for showing me how to learn to unhide and love myself.

My Goucher Girls: Melissa Arcaro, Shannon Nordlinger, Maria Ocampo, and Christina Owczarski—for helping me remember those little moments and their immense impact.

Elizabeth Arteberry, Christine Borris, Stephanie Feger, Cathy Fyock, Julie Kae, Julie Sanders Keymer, Paul Rathblott, Nicole Riggs, Truett Vaigneur, and Jason Williams, for strengthening my story with your feedback, insights, and heart. The Ignite Press Team for your support in publishing.

Jane Atkinson, Haley Foster, Suzanne Handal, Denise Harris, Erica Spooner, and Parker Taylor, for your guidance on my business and message.

Jason Williams and Jennefer Witter for first inviting me in to share my journey when I didn't even know I had a story to tell. And, the corporate partners who bring me in to amplify the diversity messages of unhiding and belonging with your teams; I keep learning from you all.

The staff and students I have mentored along the way who have challenged me to be a more reflective and inclusive leader and those who helped me build a strategic vision.

The tireless champions of disability and difference, thank you for all the work you do that forged the path and made it possible for me to see myself, be heard, and find community.

All the readers who join me on the path to unhiding and those making space for difference, many thanks to you. You allow me to continue to sparkle and feel I belong.

The Universe. I trust you implicitly.

With love, grace, kindness, and abundance.

—Ruth

SHARE THE MESSAGE FORWARD

Hey, it's Ruth here.

I hope you enjoyed *Singlehandedly* and found it both helpful and thought-provoking. I very much appreciated the opportunity to share my journey of *hiding and unhiding* with you, hoping that wherever you are on your journey, you found what you needed.

I see you.

You are now with me on this journey toward unhiding and finding ways to support others in their unhiding.

And because we realize that we can't do it alone, there are *three* initial ways you can join the *Unhiding Movement*:

> **Share a quick review.** If you are like me, you value other people's recommendations when looking for a good book to read, especially one that challenges our mindset and creates conversation.
>
> Please go to the website where you purchased this book, search for Ruth Rathblott and *Singlehandedly*, and leave a review. It's truly the greatest gift you could give me. Thank you!

Gift this book to a friend, work colleague, or family member.
If you have found this book valuable and know others who would find it helpful, consider buying them a copy as a gift. Consider sharing it with your book clubs too.
Special bulk discounts are available if you would like your whole team or organization to benefit from reading this. Just contact ruth@ruthrathblott.com.

Invite me to Speak to Your Organization
I accept a limited number of speaking and consulting engagements each year. To learn how you can bring my message to your organization, email: ruth@ruthrathblott.com or visit ruthrathblott.com.

My warmest gratitude,

Ruth

ABOUT THE AUTHOR

Inspirational speaker **Ruth Rathblott** is a TEDx speaker and an award-winning nonprofit CEO committed to creating inclusion for all. She has spent her entire career providing opportunities for those who face obstacles.

Born with a limb difference, Ruth currently speaks on issues of diversity, equity, inclusion, and belonging, the gifts of being unique, and the freedom of accepting your differences.

Ruth graduated from Miss Porter's School and holds a Bachelor of Arts degree from Goucher College and a Master of Social Work degree from Boston University. Ruth built her career leading the nonprofits Big Brothers Big Sisters of New York City and the Harlem Educational Activities Fund, which focused on mentoring youth through access to educational and volunteer programs.

She was honored as the youngest alumna ever awarded the Goucher College Excellence in Public Service Award. In 2014, Ruth was given the Smart CEO Brava Award and profiled as a CEO in *The New York Times'* Corner Office, which featured her passion and motivation for leadership. Ruth received the Trailblazer Award from the Community Resource Exchange in 2019 and the Unsung Hero Award from the Female Founders Alliance in 2020. Also in 2020, she received certification from the American Management Association in Diversity, Equity, and Inclusion. In addition to corporate speaking and consulting, Ruth also speaks for webinars and on podcasts.

Ruth resides in New York City, where she appreciates all the city offers, including Central Park, the theater, arts, and attending live sports events. Ruth thrives on travel, learning, and adventure. She serves as a board member for The Lucky Fin Project.

ruthrathblott.com

Made in the USA
Monee, IL
02 June 2023

35169234R00115